I0875888

Navigating Careers Beyond Academia

Navigating Careers Beyond Academia offers an evidence-based, step-by-step guide to successful career transition beyond academia. It provides an accessible overview of scholarship in the field of career transition, turning this into strategies for researchers to proactively pivot their careers into other sectors.

This book is designed to help readers address barriers to exploring careers beyond academia, to determine their priorities, to generate options, and to navigate some of the most persistent questions about preparing for career transition beyond academia. It guides readers through strategies for identifying relevant opportunities and communicating their skills and value effectively to potential employers, and concludes with a framework for building a career in the longer term.

Grounded in case studies of former researchers from a range of backgrounds and disciplines across STEM, social sciences, and humanities, this is a definitive guide for researchers. It also acts as a toolkit to support the work of careers consultants, researcher developers, and all involved in facilitating the professional development of doctoral and postdoctoral researchers.

Holly Prescott is a career guidance practitioner and trainer, specialising in helping doctoral and postdoctoral researchers find fulfilling careers beyond academia. She combines freelance practice with her role as Careers Adviser for Postgraduate Researchers at the University of Birmingham, UK.

Insider Guides to Success in Academia

Series Editors:
Helen Kara,
Independent Researcher, UK and
Pat Thomson,
The University of Nottingham, UK.

The *Insider Guides to Success in Academia* addresses topics too small for a full-length book on their own, but too big to cover in a single chapter or article. These topics have often been the stuff of discussions on social media, or of questions in our workshops. We designed this series to answer these questions and to provide practical support for doctoral and early career researchers. It is geared to concerns that many people experience. Readers will find these books to be companions who provide advice and help to make sense of everyday life in the contemporary university.

We have therefore:

1 invited scholars with deep and specific expertise to write. Our writers use their research and professional experience to provide well-grounded strategies to particular situations.
2 asked writers to collaborate. Most of the books are produced by writers who live in different countries, or work in different disciplines, or both. While it is difficult for any book to cover all the diverse contexts in which potential readers live and work, the different perspectives and contexts of writers goes some way to address this problem.

We understand that the use of the term 'academia' might be read as meaning the university, but we take a broader view. Pat does indeed work in a university, but spent a long time working outside of one. Helen is an independent researcher and sometimes works with universities. Both of us understand academic – or scholarly – work as now being conducted in a range of sites, from museums and the public sector to industry research and development laboratories. Academic work is also often undertaken by networks which bring together scholars in various locations. All of our writers understand that this is the case, and use the term 'academic' in this wider sense.

These books are pocket sized so that they can be carried around and visited again and again. Most of the books have a mix of examples, stories and exercises as well as explanation and advice. They are written in a collegial tone, and from a position of care as well as knowledge.

Together with our writers, we hope that each book in the series can make a positive contribution to the work and life of readers, so that you too can become insiders in scholarships.

Helen Kara, PhD FAcSS,
Independent Researcher
https://helenkara.com/
@DrHelenKara (Twitter/Insta)

Pat Thomson PhD PSM FAcSS FRSA
Professor of Education, The University of Nottingham
https://patthomson.net
@ThomsonPat

For a full list of books in the series please go to: https://www.routledge.com/Insider-Guides-to-Success-in-Academia/book-series/IGSA

Related titles in the Series include:

'Making It' as a Contract Researcher
A Pragmatic Look at Precarious Work
Nerida Spina, Jess Harris, Simon Bailey, Mhorag Goff

Navigating Academia as a Transnational Scholar from the Global South
Treasuring All the Knowledges
Roxana Chiappa Baros, Iris Viveros Avendaño

Navigating Careers Beyond Academia

A Practical Handbook for Doctoral and Postdoctoral Researchers

Holly Prescott

Routledge
Taylor & Francis Group
LONDON AND NEW YORK

Designed cover image: Getty Images

First published 2027
by Routledge
4 Park Square, Milton Park, Abingdon, Oxon OX14 4RN

and by Routledge
605 Third Avenue, New York, NY 10158

Routledge is an imprint of the Taylor & Francis Group, an informa business

British Library Cataloguing-in-Publication Data
A catalogue record for this book is available from the British Library

ISBN: 9781032965376 (hbk)
ISBN: 9781032965390 (pbk)
ISBN: 9781003589785 (ebk)

DOI: 10.4324/9781003589785

Typeset in Helvetica
by codeMantra

Contents

Acknowledgements x

Introduction 1

1 **Dealing with feelings when moving beyond academia** 15

2 **Getting started on your transition beyond academia** 37

3 **Applying your skills beyond academia** 60

4 **Tackling common questions about careers beyond academia** 85

5 **Finding and forging opportunities beyond academia** 116

6 **Communicating your value to employers beyond academia** 151

7 **Your new start beyond academia** 185

A final word 213

Index 217

Acknowledgements

This book would not have been possible without the support and stories of the many doctoral and postdoctoral researchers who it has been my privilege to support over the past ten years. Particular thanks go to Alice, Ben, Brendan, Cameron, Carlos, Cat, Emma, Ellen, Gabrielle, Hanan, Kate, Nelly, Ollie, Qiu, Sarah, Showforth, Sophie, Tania, and Victoria, who so generously offered case studies to help bring the content of this book to life.

When I first started as a specialist careers adviser for doctoral researchers, the generosity and encouragement of the career guidance and researcher development community was pivotal in helping me get to grips with the profession and start to feel like I might at some point know what I was doing. Sincere thanks to (amongst many) Catherine Reynolds, Sarah Blackford, Liz Wilkinson, Darcey Gillie, Kate Murray, Eve Uhlig, and Sharon Maguire for steering my rudder, and to the teams at AGCAS/Graduate Futures Institute and Vitae for making career guidance and researcher development such enriching professional communities of which to be a part. A big thank you also to the Careers Network and University Doctoral School teams at the University of Birmingham for trusting me with their careers provision for Postgraduate Researchers for the past 10 years.

Thanks also go to those involved in the process of getting this book out 'into the wild': to Kay Guccoine for being an advocate, to series editors Pat Thomson and Helen Kara for trusting the concept, and to Sarah Hyde,

Sophie Ganesh, Maddie Gray, and colleagues at Routledge for your support throughout. I am grateful to the peer reviewers whose feedback has helped to refine this final version, and to Sarah McLusky and David Mendes for their encouragement and endorsements as initial readers.

Huge thanks to everyone who has read and engaged with my blog 'Postgradual: The PhD Careers Blog' since its launch in 2021; your encouragement and readership have helped turn something I started on a whim one cold February Monday in lockdown into this book… and much more.

And last but not least, thank you to Matt for the encouragement (and the whimsy).

Introduction

> 'Changing your goal or your vision is ok. You can be happy beyond academia. It's not second best, it's just an alternative.'

If I could choose 22 words that I'd like every researcher to hear, it would be these. They come from an interview I did with Naomi Tyrrell, a former academic who, after more than ten years working in academia, left a permanent lectureship to begin forging a portfolio career that better suited both her own and her young family's needs. Here was someone who had achieved what some might consider to be the 'holy grail' of an open-ended academic contract, but whose priorities had changed. Her story brought home the fact that even those set on – and considered to be 'successful in' – an academic career can (and do) decide to leave.

You may be coming to this book from a similar position, or from a different one entirely. Perhaps you embarked upon your doctorate or postdoc with an academic career in mind, but decided otherwise. Perhaps you had no intention of continuing in academia after your doctoral research or your current role, but are unsure how to make the transition. Or maybe your journey here has

DOI: 10.4324/9781003589785-1

been more nuanced, and you have been forced to rethink your options. Alternatively, you may simply be unaware of the breadth of career options that could be out there for you and want to expand your possibilities. Whatever your motivation for picking up this book, evidence suggests that you're in good company.

Why explore careers beyond academia?

Data unanimously show that in many parts of the world, especially in the Global North, numbers of academic job positions have not kept pace with the growth in the number of doctorates awarded. For example, the OECD[1] report a 25% increase in the number of PhD holders within member countries between 2011 and 2021, 'with no corresponding increase in academic posts' (OECD, 2021: 78). Whilst a closer look at the data reveals significant national variations, between 2014 and 2024 the percentage of people aged 25+ who held a doctorate increased from 1.77% to 2.3% in the USA, from 1.14% to 1.82% in Australia, from 0.88% to 1.28% in the UK[2], and from 1.26% to 1.86% in Germany (UNESCO Institute for Statistics, 2025). As academia in these (and many other countries) increasingly relies on precarious contracts and permanent positions for early-career researchers remain limited, we see a structural backdrop consistent with 'an increase in the number of doctoral students' competing for a relatively constrained academic labour market (OECD, 2024: 19).

The commonly reported 'competition' for academic jobs in the Global North has further implications for academic working cultures. An international survey of over 4,000 researchers undertaken by Wellcome found that 78% agreed that high levels of competition had created 'unkind and aggressive research conditions' within their working environments (2020: 15). This culture of competition also has significant intersectional implications. For example, evidence shows that challenges in balancing paid work and caring disproportionately impact female academics, who subsequently struggle to assimilate academia's 'care-free masculinized ideals of competitive performance, 24/7 work and geographical mobility' (Ivancheva et al., 2019: 448). Furthermore, precarity has even deeper implications for those in families with additional caring responsibilities, 'of which a disproportionate number are people of colour' (Arday, 2022: 525). Studies like these give you only a glimpse of the deeper structural inequalities that many face within academia, with which you may already be all too familiar.

It therefore comes as little surprise that in her analysis of data collected 3.5 years post-graduation, Sally Hancock found that 70% of PhD graduates from UK universities had left academia by this point (2020), whilst only around 20–25% of PhD holders in the USA and Canada and just 9.5% of those in Italy land 'tenure track' academic positions (Skakni et al., 2026: 2). Despite growing disparity between supply and demand for doctoral graduates within academia, however, increased recruitment of doctoral students has become key to many universities' strategic goals (e.g. Kim and Spencer-Oatey, 2021: 917), meaning that whilst funding conditions, political decisions, and other economic factors result in shrinking academic job markets, institutions nevertheless continue to grow their doctoral student numbers. As a researcher, therefore, it's fair to say that you sit at a complex crossroads between institutional and governmental agendas. Hence, when those agendas shift or clash, the job market – and the options you find yourself navigating – can shift with them.

Even if an academic career has long been your goal, understanding wider options is a pragmatic move, enhancing your ability to adjust your plans in the face of widespread uncertainty, inequity, and political and economic change. Assessing other options could even be a means of realising your full potential, especially if the workload of a more senior academic, in which research and teaching give way to grant writing, people management, and admin, isn't for you. This is why, reflecting on her own career transition beyond academia, Melissa Dalgleish recommends that researchers figure out 'what you really love about academia and think about jobs that will let you do those things most of the time. [...] That might be an academic job. Or it might not' (2018: 16).

On the other hand, it may be that moving beyond academia has long been part of your plan. This is the case for many researchers I meet, whose desire to work in other sectors is often motivated by 'pull factors' such as better salaries, access to better resources, and the opportunity to do work with a more concrete impact (e.g. Kallio et al. 2024). Even if you always intended on taking your experience beyond academia, that doesn't mean you should automatically know exactly which options will suit you best and how to pursue these. Taking time to explore the possibilities could reveal potential career ideas you haven't previously considered, or widen your search beyond the 'obvious' options for someone with your background and experience.

Exploring careers beyond academia isn't 'failure' or 'selling out,' but is part of the process of finding what feels right for you. Exploring your career options more widely doesn't necessarily mean that you are straying from a path that you 'ought to' follow, nor does it mean that you are alone. Rather, you are taking initiative and opening yourself up to the possibilities taken by many before, simultaneous to, and after you. The other piece of good news is that exploring career options requires curiosity and research skills, so as a researcher you are well-placed to uncover a range of possibilities open to you in other sectors. This book is here to support you with this: to provide a structure to help you apply your enquiring mind and research skills to investigating your next steps, and to equip you with career management skills that you can apply throughout your professional life.

Using this book

Chapter 1 focuses on recognising common mental and emotional barriers to career exploration beyond academia, offering practical tips for spotting and managing such challenges. **Chapter 2** focuses on how to get started with your career transition, contesting the notion of linear career 'paths' and reimagining your career as an incremental process of 'tweaking' your professional activities to align with your priorities. **Chapter 3** guides you through the process of generating ideas for career options linked to your skills and interests, whilst **Chapter 4** tackles some of the most common questions about preparing for career transition beyond academia and deciding which types of opportunities will be your focus. Once you've got your ideas about the types of opportunities, sectors, or employers that you are going to target, Chapters 5 and 6 talk you through the practicalities of identifying relevant opportunities and communicating your value effectively in recruitment processes. **Chapter 5** outlines common recruitment methods used by employers beyond academia and what you can do to devise an effective 'mixed methods' job hunt; **Chapter 6** focuses on communicating your skills in ways that resonate with employers, helping to overcome stumbling blocks such as employers' preconceptions of researchers and concerns around overqualification. Finally, **Chapter 7** looks beyond the recruitment process, helping you to navigate your new working environment and use your next role beyond academia to build for the longer term.

With the exception of Chapter 4 which is structured around a range of frequently asked questions relating to career transition beyond academia, each chapter comprises five sections. The first section ('What's the Evidence?') uses research and scholarship to highlight key findings to inform your own journey. The second section ('What Does This Mean for You?') translates these findings into potential challenges and opportunities, introducing ideas on how to mitigate and leverage these. Section three ('Get to Work') then presents practical exercises or frameworks to put your learning from each chapter into action, many of which are tried and tested in my ten years of career guidance practice supporting doctoral and postdoctoral researchers. The fourth section ('Case Study') then gives at least one example to help you see the advice contained in each chapter 'in action.' Finally, each chapter ends with a summary list of key takeaways.

Whilst care has been taken throughout this book to include case studies representing a range of academic backgrounds and career areas, it simply isn't possible to include examples from every single subject area or sector. When considering the case studies, resist the urge to dismiss those from contributors outside of your immediate research area and sector interests, and instead try to focus on how to apply some of the tips and strategies shared to your own career transition.

In terms of *when* to use this book, it can be all too easy to put off thinking about next steps until the end of your doctorate or current contract. This book doesn't promise a 'quick fix': it is designed to help you develop the mindsets required for career transition beyond academia, through thoughtful engagement. Spreading the activities across your doctorate or current contract will therefore give you the time needed to reflect, act, and refine your job search, rather than trying to cram the whole career transition cycle into a panicked few months. Plus, job search timelines can vary significantly by sector. Whilst some roles (like graduate programmes) hire almost a year in advance, fluctuating economic conditions may mean that job hunting takes longer than expected, so starting early gives you flexibility. The outline below suggests how to map the activities in this book to different stages of your research journey.

- **As early as possible:**
  - Identify and address any mental or emotional barriers you may be experiencing around exploring careers beyond academia (Chapter 1).
  - Start to determine what you want from your next steps (Chapter 2).
- **Mid-stage of your doctorate/ contract:**
  - Look 'beyond the obvious' to generate career ideas linked to your skills and interests (Chapter 3).

  - Take structured action, trying things out and talking to people to research options and build your network (Chapters 4 and 5). Building a meaningful network involves developing trust over time, not swooping in late on and asking for a job!
  - Revisit the priorities you identified in Chapter 2 in light of your conversations, actions, and how your research is progressing.

- **Latter stage of your doctorate/ contract:**
  - Devise your mixed-methods job hunt and translate your experience for potential employers (Chapter 6).
  - Prepare for your transition (Chapter 7).

- **If you're already near the end:**
  - If you are already short on time and are imminently coming to the end of your programme or grant, or are facing redundancy, don't panic; it's never too late to take meaningful steps.
  - Prioritise the 'keep/lose/add' exercise in Chapter 2, to give you direction or to check if options you are considering align with what you want.
  - If you are still struggling to focus on your job hunt at this late stage, use the 'what does this mean for you' section of Chapter 5 for tips, then the 'get to work' section for practical strategies for finding and forging opportunities.
  - Focus in on Chapter 6's guidance around conveying yourself to employers in a convincing way. Remember, no first role beyond academia is forever, but it can be a stepping stone towards longer-term goals.
  - If you're still struggling, head back to Chapter 1 to see if there are deeper issues you need to tackle before starting on your transition.

A note on terminology

Unless quoting a study, article, or case study contributor using different terminology, this book uses the terms 'doctoral researchers' and 'postdoctoral researchers' to describe its main audience. This is to remain inclusive of readers pursuing doctoral research other than a PhD, and to avoid terms which may be more country-specific (for example, 'postgraduate researcher' or 'PGR' in the UK, 'higher degree by research' or 'HDR' in Australia, 'graduate student' in the US and Canada). Whilst the term 'Early Career Researchers' could be used to describe those undertaking research at both doctoral and postdoctoral levels, in the UK (at least), the term may not resonate with readers still undertaking doctoral work. As a result, doctoral and postdoctoral researchers are referred to distinctly in order to convey relevance to both. Beyond these groups however, the content of this book is also likely to be relevant to readers looking to transition from longer-term academic positions, as well as those moving from other academic roles such as short-term teaching contracts.

Justifying the choice of terminology for the kinds of careers covered by this book is more complex. It is difficult to describe work other than academic research or teaching without creating a false dichotomy between 'academic' and 'non-academic' careers. I have actively avoided the terms 'non-academic careers' or 'careers outside of academia' since this book showcases many individuals whose careers remain linked to, and involved with, academic activities and environments. Instead, I have chosen to use the phrases 'careers beyond academia' and 'other sectors.' 'Careers beyond academia' is used with the intention of showing that careers can reach 'beyond' academia without completely detaching from academic activities and environments. Meanwhile, 'other sectors' is used to move away from terminology that places academia at the centre, to emphasise that other sectors are not inferior to academia, but are simply different.

Preparing to explore

As you begin exploring what could be out there for you beyond academia, remember: career ideas, like research ideas, don't come out of nowhere. Chances are that the focus for your doctoral or postdoctoral research didn't come to you in a sudden epiphany, but rather grew from your contact with ideas, people, experiences, and existing work. Perhaps your research evolved out of your previous academic work, such as Master's or undergraduate study. Perhaps it was inspired by your experience in a current or previous job. Your research ideas may even have emerged from personal lived experiences, or other projects such as community work, campaigning, or activism. Alternatively, you may have taken a project because that was what was on offer in your chosen field at the time. Just as your research ideas didn't come out of nowhere, neither will your ideas for whatever you do next.

Table 0.1 outlines some common methods of generating research ideas, and translates these into methods for generating career ideas, along with example actions that you can take to set your career discovery in motion.

As the examples in Table 0.1 show, coming up with ideas for both the focus of your research and for your next career move are *processes* that often take place over time. Consequently, the example career planning actions listed are things that you can do from an early stage in your doctorate or postdoc to avoid panic and indecision when you reach the end.

Table 0.1 Translating methods for generating research ideas into methods for exploring career options

Research ideas are generated through...	*Career ideas are generated through...*	*Equivalent actions you can take to explore options...*
Work that you have previously done (academic or otherwise): things you enjoyed; problems you want to solve.	Work that you have previously done (academic or otherwise): reflecting on what you enjoyed and didn't enjoy, and what you'd like to do more of.	Write down a list of activities you've enjoyed most during your PhD or postdoc so far, and those you've enjoyed least. Use the 'keep, lose, add' exercise in Chapter 2 to help with this, and to see how it can link to career options.
Talking to people, e.g. relevant experts, other people in your discipline, professionals in your field, etc.	Talking to people, e.g. people working in organisations, roles, or sectors that interest you.	Identify people doing types of work that might interest you and see if they'd be happy to chat about what they do. Use the LinkedIn research techniques and networking scripts outlined in Chapters 3 and 4 to help with this.

(*Continued*)

Table 0.1 (Continued)

Research ideas are generated through...	*Career ideas are generated through...*	*Equivalent actions you can take to explore options...*
Engaging with existing work and ideas: reading previous work in the field to work out what your research will contribute.	Engaging with existing work and ideas: learning about what other doctoral graduates have done, what is out there, and where you might contribute.	Build up a picture of what previous doctoral graduates or former postdocs from your subject area have gone on to do. Use the LinkedIn research techniques like the alumni search outlined in Chapter 3 to help with this.
Your personal experience, values, and motivations.	Your personal experience, values, and motivations.	Identify companies or organisations who work towards goals linked to your values and motivations. These could be potential future employers to research further.
Taking on a project that is already defined, happens to be available, or is given to you, rather than one you actively designed or chose.	Taking opportunities that are realistically available to you right now to 'try things out.'	Take advantage of opportunities that come up (e.g. an internship, a committee role, etc.); reflect on what you learned from these about your preferences, strengths, and constraints, and what this tells you about what you want from your next step.

Now that your career curiosity cogs are turning, it's time to put you at the centre; to work out not just what you *can* do after a doctorate or postdoc in your subject area, but to understand what you *want* to do, and take practical steps towards this.

Notes

1 The Organisation for Economic Co-operation and Development (OECD) is a forum focused on sustainable economic growth and comprises 38 countries, all considered to be 'developed' democratic nations with market-based economies across Europe, North America, Central America, South America, Asia, and Oceania.
2 In the UK, the latest available figure is from 2021 rather than 2024.

References

Arday, J. (2022) '"More to prove and more to lose": race, racism and precarious employment in higher education,' *British Journal of Sociology of Education*, 43(4), pp. 513–533. doi: 10.1080/01425692.2022.2074375.

Dalgleish, M. (2018) 'The things I wish I'd known during my PhD,' in Fruscione, J. and Baker, K. J. (eds.) *Succeeding Outside the Academy: Career Paths beyond the Humanities, Social Sciences and STEM*. 1st edn. Lawrence: Kansas University Press, pp. 11–22.

Hancock, S. (2020) 'The employment of PhD graduates in the UK: what do we know?', *Higher Education Policy Institute* [Blog]. Available at: https://www.hepi.ac.uk/2020/02/17/the-employment-of-phd-graduates-in-the-uk-what-do-we-know/ [Accessed 2 February 2025].

Ivancheva, M., Lynch, K. and Keating, K. (2019) 'Precarity, gender and care in the neoliberal academy,' *Gender, Work & Organization*, 26(4), pp. 448–462. doi: 10.1111/gwao.12350.

Kallio, T., Siekkinen, T., Pekkola, E., Kivistö, J., Nokkala, T. and Kuoppakangas, P. (2024) 'Push and pull factors affecting in leaving academia,' *Tertiary Education and Management*, 30, pp. 65–80. doi: 10.1007/s11233-024-09135-4.

Kim, K.H. and Spencer-Oatey, H. (2021) 'Enhancing the recruitment of postgraduate researchers from diverse countries: managing the application process,' *Higher Education*, 82, pp. 917–935. doi: 10.1007/s10734-021-00681-z.

OECD (2021) *Reducing the Precarity of Academic Research Careers*. OECD Science, Technology and Industry Policy Papers, No. 113. Paris: OECD Publishing. doi: 10.1787/0f8bd468-en.

OECD (2024) *The State of Academic Careers in OECD Countries – An Evidence Review.* OECD Education Policy Perspectives, No. 91. Paris: OECD Publishing. doi: 10.1787/ea9d3108-en

Skakni, I., Kereselidze, N., Parmentier, M., Delobbe, N. and Inouye, K. (2026). 'PhD graduates pursuing careers beyond academia: a scoping review,' *Higher Education Research & Development*, pp. 1–20. doi: 10.1080/07294360.2025.2515211.

UNESCO Institute for Statistics (UIS) (2025). *Educational Attainment Rate, Completed Doctoral or Equivalent Education, Population 25+ years, Both Sexes*. Available at: https://databrowser.uis.unesco.org/browser/EDUCATION/UIS-SDG4Monitoring/t4.4/i4.4.3 [Accessed 12 December 2025].

Wellcome (2020) *What Researchers Think of the Culture They Work in*. London: Wellcome. Available at: https://wellcome.org/insights/reports/what-researchers-think-about-research-culture [Accessed 7 July 2024].

1 Dealing with feelings when moving beyond academia

As well as the practical aspects of career transition, how we feel about making a career move – our hopes, fears, and reservations – can profoundly impact how we approach the process. Whilst many of the researchers I support usually begin by asking where to look for jobs or how to create a 'non-academic' CV, once we get talking, it's common for deeper issues to surface, including:

- Feeling overwhelmed by the idea of 'starting again' after spending years focused on a specific research area.
- Worries that they will be letting others (or themselves) down if they don't stay in academia.
- Lack of support from others in exploring careers beyond academia.
- Difficulty 'seeing themselves' as anything other than an academic.
- Feeling they are 'giving up' by turning down further short-term research or teaching contracts.

No matter how many job board links you collect, or how many tips you gather for crafting a winning CV, the likelihood that you will act on this information is low if you are

DOI: 10.4324/9781003589785-2

experiencing mental and emotional barriers like these. To act upon any practical information, advice, and guidance about considering wider career options, you need to be in the right mindset to do so and to acknowledge what might be holding you back. To help with this, let's start by summarising what the evidence says about these kinds of mental 'blockers' before working out what you can do to manage them.

What's the evidence?

Moving beyond academia can feel energising and hopeful, but may also bring doubt, pressures, and mixed emotions. Even if this shift has always been part of your plan, for instance, you may still feel hesitant about how others may respond once you start to share and act on your decision. And if you do encounter negative attitudes from others, knowing you are not alone can help you manage the emotional side of the transition. For example, if we look at research in this field, studies do show instances in which doctoral supervisors and advisers have been found to encourage academic research careers 'while being less encouraging of other career paths,' creating stress for those who feel unable to 'live up to the expectations of their advisors' (Sauermann and Roach, 2012: 5). More specifically, a study of postdocs in the US revealed instances in which pursuits related to careers in other sectors were viewed as a 'distraction' or were even actively opposed by managers (Hayter and Parker, 2019: 564). Some participants felt they were treated differently by management for considering such careers; one described this attitude as 'you are dead to me,' whilst others admitted having to lie to management to secure time to attend other-sector career events (563). Even when academic staff believe such views are outmoded, some still report attitudes within their departments that researchers who shift their careers beyond academia are viewed 'as failures and embarrassments to the profession' (Zimmerman, 2018: 16): an opinion which unjustly dismisses not only tough academic labour markets but also the wide variety of motivations to undertake doctoral and postdoctoral work in the first place.

It's also common to be apprehensive about how moving on from academia might impact your sense of identity. Research in the field of work transition shows that experiences such as redundancy, or loss of a 'valued position,' can leave you having to navigate a 'liminal state' between letting go of your previous professional identity and assimilating a new one (Conroy and O'Leary-Kelly, 2014: 67). If you consider an academic career to be a 'valued position,' then 'losing' this position through the revision of your career plans can leave you having to 'let go' of your imagined academic future and refocus your professional identity around different goals. Whilst evidence shows that some people emerge from such experiences with an even more authentic sense of identity, it also highlights the risk of being 'cognitively and emotionally consumed' by the loss, impeding the ability to move on (69). This might help explain why around 20% of the participants in Hayter and Parker's study referenced above said that realising academia was no longer a long-term option for them led to feelings of 'existential crisis' (2019: 563). However, moving beyond academia doesn't necessarily mean 'overwriting' your former self with a new one, but is more likely to involve renegotiating your professional identity so that your 'researcher-self is always present and becomes part of a new, reconstructed identity' (Li and Horta, 2024: 431). Understanding the key skills and lessons you want to take with you from academia into your next steps is therefore crucial, rather than dwelling solely on what you feel you are leaving behind.

Spending years on postdoctoral contracts can further complicate feelings about moving on from academia. Evidence shows that if you're finding it difficult to step away from fixed-term academic roles, you may be experiencing 'cruel optimism': a paradox in which something you desire also poses an obstacle to your flourishing (Berlant, 2011: 1). For example, a study of precariously employed academics in Australia found that many were chasing scraps of short-term work, hoping that these would turn into something more stable (Bone, 2021). Participants reported feeling stuck in a cycle where even 'minor "wins"' like incrementally longer contracts at least made them feel that they were moving forwards and gave hope of securing a longer-term position, whilst leaving academia would mean surrendering this hope (282). Research also shows the extreme measures that some precariously employed academics will go to in order to break this cycle of cruel optimism, including moving overseas or taking long trips to physically remove the temptation to accept further temporary academic work (McKenzie, 2021: 533). It follows, that spending years on fixed-term contracts, accruing experience and credentials that ultimately do not lead to a permanent position, can understandably undermine your sense of agency over your career. If exploring alternative careers feels like giving up hope, turning down short-term income feels too risky, or you have little faith that your professional efforts will have the desired outcome, then your motivation to look into other options may understandably suffer.

Moving on from academia can therefore be psychologically and emotionally complex, and with it may also come anger at being 'pushed out' of the system, along with a sense of injustice both for yourself and for others. To prepare to explore your options more widely, it's crucial to acknowledge such psychological and emotional barriers and to spot any that may be relevant for you. However, before we address these barriers, it's reassuring to highlight what research shows about researchers' career outcomes beyond this often-fraught transition period.

Whilst some studies report lower levels of satisfaction amongst doctorate holders working in other sectors compared to those in academia (e.g. Di Paolo, 2016), others find no such correlation (e.g. Lawson and Lopes-Bento, 2024; Spronken-Smith et al., 2024). In the UK specifically, data show average career satisfaction for doctoral graduates to be similar for those working in academia (94.2%) and those working elsewhere (92.8%) (Hancock, 2023: 1532). However, the type of role undertaken appears crucial, with participants working in research-based roles beyond academia reporting a higher level of job satisfaction (95.7%) than those in academia (Hancock, 2023: 1532).

This pattern emerges in other studies too, in which doctorate holders working beyond academia experience higher job satisfaction when their roles still involve an element of research (e.g. Alfano et al., 2021; Hnatkova et al., 2022). This suggests that finding work that uses skills developed within academia is key to professional fulfilment for many researchers who have moved into other sectors. In this respect, it's encouraging to see that research does show examples of doctoral graduates working beyond academia who feel immersed by and committed to their work, find meaning in their roles, and invest in their professional development (Garcia-Morante et al., 2025: 7), and who express pleasant surprise at their enjoyment of their work post career transition, both in academic administration (Ewing-Cooper and Gallien, 2022) and in sectors beyond academia (Spronken-Smith et al., 2024).

Evidence also warns against jumping to conclusions about how academic supervisors and managers may respond to your interest in exploring other-sector careers. For instance, a recent UK study of doctoral supervisors revealed that despite reporting greater pride if one of their students were to pursue an academic career, most expressed a desire to support their doctoral researchers to develop the career that was right for them, regardless of sector (Buckland et al., 2024). In this study, factors such as lack of awareness, experience, time, and confidence were the most common barriers that supervisors experienced to discussing wider career ideas with their doctoral researchers. If you do face ambivalence from supervisors or managers around your interest in moving beyond academia, this could be down to their awareness of their own limitations rather than outright disapproval or judgement.

What does this mean for you?

If fear, overwhelm, anger, or low confidence are holding you back from embracing alternative career options, you are by no means alone. Through recognising these feelings, you can start to work through them and engage in wider career exploration with a more open mind. Even if you feel excited about taking your next steps beyond academia, you may still be apprehensive. Finishing your doctorate or postdoc, or deciding to leave your academic contract, is by no means 'the end,' but can often feel like a kind of ending: the ending of a period of intense and focused labour, for example, or the ending of your deep association with a particular research group or academic field.

Exercise 1.1 is designed to help you identify any thoughts that may be holding you back from exploring wider career options, assess the validity of these thoughts, and turn them into more constructive thoughts to increase your motivation for exploring your next steps. Tackling these thoughts, and the feelings they provoke, early in your career transition can also help you to avoid becoming 'stuck' in behaviours like:

- 'Talking yourself out' of opportunities once you start to job hunt.
- Putting pressure on yourself to make the 'right career decision,' leading to decision paralysis.
- Applying for (further) postdocs or other academic jobs 'by default' because you feel like that's what you should be doing, or because you don't want to feel like you're giving up.
- Resenting the need to explore careers beyond academia.
- 'Burying your head in the sand' and avoiding taking action.

Beyond addressing negative thoughts, the above also suggests that a key factor in tackling emotional and psychological barriers to career change is gaining support, both from others and – importantly – from yourself. Some studies showed how judgement from others, and ensuing feelings of shame and guilt, impacted participants' engagement with broader career options. If you feel those around you aren't on board with your plans, this can, in turn, diminish your trust in your own decisions. On top of this are potential feelings of identity loss or crisis: after years of work in a particular research field, it can be difficult to see yourself as anything other than an ancient historian, an organic chemist, a classicist, or whatever academic moniker has come to define you and your work. To move on from academia, and to avoid becoming consumed by identity loss, you need to be able to tell a convincing story about your decision to explore wider options. Herminia Ibarra notes the connection between career change, identity shift, and gaining others' backing, saying that it is through 'making public declarations about what we seek and what common thread binds our old and new selves' that we 'clarify our [career] intentions' and 'improve our ability to enlist others' support' for our new career goals (2003: 157).

Exercise 1.2 helps you devise a self-narrative to nurture your own and others' understanding of your choice to consider broader career options. It is designed to show that deciding to do something other than academic research and teaching doesn't necessarily mean cutting all ties with your academic self; instead, it focuses on helping you identify the consistencies between your academic experience so far and what you will go on to do next. You are not 'giving up' or 'failing': you are simply taking your experience and what you have learned from this into a new chapter, as some of the research we saw above emphasised.

The narrative – or 'support statement' – that you devise in Exercise 1.2 can be useful in several ways. First, if you feel your supervisor(s) or manager(s) will be open to your wishes to explore wider career options, you can use it to start a conversation around how they may be able to support you. If this is not the case, your statement can still help you to consolidate your decision and advocate for yourself in the face of resistance from others. For example, when confronted by a senior academic as to whether I felt I was 'wasting my brain' by deciding to focus on career options beyond academia, I found my support statement (outlined below) valuable as an articulate response to their reasoning, as much to reassure myself as to try to get them on side. That was my story, and I was sticking to it.

Take time now to work through the exercises and address any thoughts and emotions that may be holding you back, clearing your mental space ready for exploration and action.

Get to work

Exercise 1.1: What's stopping you?

Use Table 1.1 to record any negative thoughts that you are experiencing about careers beyond academia and your ability to explore these. Use the columns in the table to:

- Express each negative thought.
- Write down any evidence you have that counters each thought.
- Note actions you could take if each thought came true.
- Use the evidence and the actions to reframe each negative thought into a more positive thought.

Table 1.1 Reframing negative thoughts around careers beyond academia

Negative thought	*Evidence against the thought*	*Is there anything you can do?*	*More positive thought*
If I don't go for academic jobs, this means I'm a failure.	My old lab mate moved into industry and I do not think they are a failure. Whatever I do, my partner is proud of me and supports me. There are many structural factors involved.	If a supervisor believes this and reacts very badly, I can ask someone else for a reference. I can define what 'success' means for me personally.	For me, success means a good work/life balance. Applying for the right jobs beyond academia will help me to succeed in this. If I don't go for academic jobs, I am choosing a valid alternative for my professional life.
If I leave academia, I might end up in a job that I hate.	I know other people who work outside of academia and are happy in their jobs.	If I don't like my first job beyond academia, I can use the experience to apply for other things.	My first job beyond academia won't be forever. It is my first step. I can choose to do something else if I don't enjoy it.

(*Continued*)

Table 1.1 (Continued)

Negative thought	*Evidence against the thought*	*Is there anything you can do?*	*More positive thought*
I've been working on contracts to build academic experience for years; if I move on now, all this time will have been wasted.	I have gained a lot of skills and developed as person during my academic work. There are things I wouldn't be so good at if I hadn't had this experience.	If I move my career beyond academia and feel like my time in academia was wasted, I can use this experience to find work that better uses the abilities I gained from academia. If I feel like I wasted my time in academia, I can seek support to help me be kinder to myself and understand why I made the decisions I made.	I can focus on finding opportunities beyond academia that allow me to apply experience, skills, knowledge etc. that I developed during my academic work.

Exercise 1.2: Your support statement

Use the 'support statement' template in Box 1.1 to construct your own narrative about why you are choosing to explore, or are prioritising, career options beyond academia. In the first part which asks you to reflect on what you have enjoyed in academia, try to be as specific as possible. Rather than choosing broad activities like 'teaching' or 'lab work,' think about what it is you actually enjoy about those things, e.g. 'explaining concepts

> **Box 1.1 Your support statement**
>
> **During my time in academia, I have really enjoyed**
>
> ______________________________
>
> ______________________________
>
> ______________________________
>
> **I have learned a lot about myself, including** ______
>
> ______________________________
>
> ______________________________
>
> ______________________________
>
> **Consequently, I am now looking for opportunities that will allow me to** ______________
>
> ______________________________
>
> ______________________________
>
> ______________________________

in an accessible way,' or 'identifying and troubleshooting technical problems,' or 'turning messy data into something useful.' Exercise 2.1 in Chapter 2 offers some further pointers on how to break this down.

You can use this support statement to clarify what you are looking for from your next step, as well as using it in conversations with others to support your choice to explore other options. To give you an example, in Box 1.2 I share how my support statement would have looked as I came towards the end of my doctorate.

Box 1.2 My support statement

During my time in academia, I have really enjoyed: *any work that has been people-facing (especially student-facing), including teaching, delivering outreach seminars, and leading campus tours on open days. I've enjoyed presenting my work, and pretty much any public speaking opportunity I've had during my PhD.*

I have learned a lot about myself, including: *that I thrive in a university environment, but that I don't cope well working in isolation, or with the uncertainty of having to find my own funding, the stress of which impacts on my enjoyment and quality of work.*

Consequently, I am now looking for opportunities that will allow me to: *stay in a university or research institute environment where I'm helping people to learn and develop, where I'm regularly presenting in front of people, but where I don't have the pressure of having to bring in the funding to keep my own job.*

Case study

This section features two stories from real researchers who took their careers in directions other than full-time, permanent academic positions. Each shows lived experience of issues we have discussed in this chapter.

Tania's story in case study 1.1 shows that rather than feeling 'wasted' beyond academia, she found a path where her abilities were valued, and reframed her career move in a way that works for her. Tania also challenges the binary of 'academic' and 'other' careers, combining academic research interests with 'academic adjacent' work.

Gabrielle's story in case study 1.2 shows the importance of solidarity and community in her navigation of career transition, and in refiguring her professional identity. For Gabrielle, finding a supportive and psychologically safe environment to talk about careers beyond academia was key. At the end of this chapter, you can find a list of communities designed to support and unite people looking to shift their careers beyond academia.

Case study 1.1 Tania's story

After two years of short-term teaching work and six years on fixed-term postdoc research contracts in the humanities, Tania decided it was time to make a change. She says:

'It's hard for me to tell whether it was destiny or desperation. I was in my mid-30s, and we had just moved to a new city with a mortgage, a one-year-old, and no family support in place. I had interviewed for two long-term lectureship positions and was offered neither, but came "runner up" for both. I had thought I would feel despair upon hearing this news, but instead I felt...relief. I took it as a sign to stop anxiously applying for academic jobs.

Academia no longer seemed like the land of milk and honey. I had done a PhD, two years on bitty teaching contracts, and six years on prestigious funded postdoctoral fellowships, for the first of which I spent two years travelling between Canada and the UK as I had just started dating my now-husband. However, I was no closer to job security. And yet I felt overwhelmed at the prospect of *not* being an academic: since the age of 16 I had thought I would be a professor, and if I wasn't an academic, who was I?

I felt like a failure and academic friends passed on condolences, my exiting perceived as a tragedy. On top of this, I felt very insecure and overwhelmed about applying for non-academic jobs. I had some support from career coaches, but it was personal connections that helped me clarify a new path. My husband was working at a university in a non-academic role, and a colleague of his had recently moved into "research support." I had no idea what this entailed, but my husband suggested I speak to his colleague to find out.

Like me, the colleague also had a humanities PhD, and was enjoying his role supporting academics with external funding applications. He then introduced me to his line manager who I took out for coffee; she explained the skills needed in this line of work, I explained my own background, and she said that with my transferable skills and academic experience I was like "gold dust". I tried not to cry, being so unused to feeling valuable. A few weeks later a vacancy opened in her team, and I was appointed to a short-term role covering someone else's secondment, which although precarious felt like a positive new path for me. I even turned down another postdoctoral role with a big commute. I needed to try something different, for my family and for myself. My values had changed, and with them, my priorities.

I have re-framed my career move as not leaving academia *per se*, but as simply occupying another room. I describe myself as an "alt-ac" (alternative-academic). I have won grants as an independent researcher and am currently writing my second monograph. This is tricky while working full-time and having caring responsibilities, but it's important to me to do the research and to model a different way of performing academic work. Leaving an academic job doesn't have to mean leaving research or academia altogether. I love what I do now, enabling others to succeed and focus on the research they feel passionate about. I continue to feel that I am a valuable member of the research community and higher education, the salary and hours are terrific, and continuing my own research – in my time and on my own terms – makes it all even better!'

Case study 1.2 Gabrielle's story

Gabrielle completed a PhD in Social Psychology, then one postdoc and six years in a tenure-track academic role, all in the US. She shares her story of how creating community helped her shift her career beyond academia:

'My PhD was on prejudice and stereotyping, particularly related to the LGBTQ+ community. When I started it, I had no intention of becoming an academic; my goal was actually to work in policy research. A few years into my PhD, I fell in love with teaching. I completed a policy research internship which was fun, but I decided to lean in to teaching and shifted gears to aim for a career in academia. Initially I landed a one-year postdoc which meant moving across the country. After that, I was offered a tenure-track academic position at a small women's liberal arts college where I taught for six years. I loved much of my time there. I had amazing students and faculty colleagues, but changes handed down from administration started to erode morale and shift the values and priorities of the institution, so I left and landed a job in research at a non-profit. My work fell under programme evaluation, focusing on improving internal processes. About 18 months later, I shifted to a new company where I continue to work in programme evaluation and policy research. Both of my jobs beyond academia so far have been remote, working for companies based outside of my state.

For me, if you are considering a career change out of academia, community is key. You are incredibly smart and good at learning new things, so you can learn what kind of jobs you might be best suited for and how to write a good application. What I found much harder was trying to navigate the identity shift and other psychological processes alone. Initially, I didn't know anyone who had left a tenured or tenure-track academic position. I felt very isolated and started exploring LinkedIn to learn about job searching. I ended up connecting with several other academics at my university who were also job searching. We formed a small support group and started meeting weekly to provide each other with both material support (help with applications, interview advice, etc.) and emotional support. I started seeing more transitioning academics on LinkedIn, so I posted about starting a free peer support group. A dozen or so people responded, and we met on Zoom. A group member suggested the name "Recovering Academics," and we set up a weekly meeting time and a Slack workspace. The group now has a membership of nearly 400 and we have members at every level, from students to professors, based in a variety of locations. They all share similar stories and tips around job hunting beyond academia, and many stay in the group both to give support to others and to continue to process ongoing issues that come up once they land new jobs. There are several similar groups springing up, so look for ones near you or that you can participate in remotely. If you can't find any, start one! Being with other people who 'get it' really makes a difference.'

Takeaways

- Before exploring options and job hunting, it is important to acknowledge any emotional or psychological barriers that may impact your motivation to engage with career options beyond academia.
- Research shows that it is common for doctoral and postdoctoral researchers to encounter negative attitudes towards their decision to explore wider career options. This can understandably lead to feelings of fear, guilt, and shame.
- Moving on from academia can feel both daunting and liberating. It can be difficult to envision yourself as anything other than a sociologist/a linguist/a theoretical physicist, etc., and time spent on fixed-term contracts may impact your sense of agency over your career. However, research suggests that most doctoral and postdoctoral researchers find good levels of job satisfaction beyond academia.
- Reframing negative and unhelpful thoughts about moving on from academia can help you to avoid counterproductive behaviour patterns that may impede your career transition.
- Devising a narrative about what you have learned from your academic (and other) experience and what this tells you about your priorities going forward can be useful, both in gaining support from others and in helping you start to envision an alternative future.
- You are not alone in your ambitions to take your career beyond academia; seeking out others in the same position can help you feel less isolated and provide a psychologically safe place to discuss ideas and actions.

Useful resources

The following list outlines some existing online communities focused on supporting career moves beyond academia:

- **AltAc Careers** – a supportive group for people who have transitioned out of academia or are thinking about it: www.facebook.com/groups/altaccareersuk/
- **Compassionate Cohort** – an online gathering space for former (and current) academics navigating the logistics and the emotional landscape of moving beyond academia: https://compassionatecohort.my.canva.site/
- **PhD Paths** – includes a bank of informational interviews with doctoral graduates who have moved into a range of sectors: https://www.phdpaths.co/
- **The Professor is Out** – community for people looking to move, or in the process of moving, beyond academia: www.facebook.com/groups/professorisout
- **Research Careers** – a bank of profiles showcasing the stories of doctoral graduates now working in academic-adjacent roles and sectors beyond academia: https://research-careers.org/
- **Researching.io** – an online mentoring community matching academic researchers with doctorate holders working in other sectors: https://www.researching.io/

References

Alfano, V., Gaeta, G. and Pinto, M. (2021) 'Non-academic employment and matching satisfaction among PhD graduates with high intersectoral mobility potential,' *International Journal of Manpower*, 42(7), pp. 1202–1223. doi: 10.1108/IJM-10-2020-0489.

Berlant, L. (2011) *Cruel Optimism*. Durham, NC: Duke University Press.

Bone, K.D. (2021) 'Cruel optimism and precarious employment: the crisis ordinariness of academic work,' *Journal of Business Ethics*, 174(2), pp. 275–290. doi: 10.1007/s10551-020-04605-2.

Buckland, N., Richardson, K. and Ehata, R. (2024) 'Applying Behaviour Change Theory to Understand PhD Supervisors' Barriers and Enablers to Supporting PhD Students with Academic and Other-Sector Careers,' *Qeios*. doi: 10.32388/Y2S1I9.2.

Conroy, S.A. and O'Leary-Kelly, A.M. (2014) 'Letting go and moving on: work-related identity loss and recovery,' *The Academy of Management Review*, 39(1), pp. 67–87. doi: 10.5465/amr.2011.0396.

Di Paolo, A. (2016) '(Endogenous) Occupational choices and job satisfaction among recent Spanish PhD recipients,' *International Journal of Manpower*, 37, pp. 511–535. doi: 10.1108/ijm-10-2014-0197.

Ewing-Cooper, A. and Gallien, K.N. (2022) 'Off the tenure track: experiences of PhD graduates in academic administrative positions,' *Perspectives: Policy and Practice in Higher Education*, 26(3), pp. 102–108. doi: 10.1080/13603108.2021.2012720.

Garcia-Morante, M., Sundström, L., Pyhältö, K. and Castelló, M. (2025). 'Transitioning beyond Academia: engagement and disengagement experiences of HASS PhD holders,' *Studies in Higher Education*, pp. 1–16. doi: 10.1080/03075079.2025.2468849

Hancock, S. (2023) 'Knowledge or science-based economy? The employment of UK PhD graduates in research roles beyond academia,' *Studies in Higher Education*, 48(10), pp. 1523–1537. doi: 10.1080/03075079.2023.2249023.

Hayter, C. and Parker, M. (2019) 'Factors that influence the transition of university postdocs to non-academic scientific careers: an exploratory study,' *Research Policy*, 48(3), pp. 556–570. doi: 10.1016/j.respol.2018.09.009.

Hnatkova, E., Degtyarova, I., Kersschot, M. and Boman, J. (2022) 'Labour market perspectives for PhD graduates in Europe,' *European Journal of Education*, 57, pp. 395–409. doi: 10.1111/ejed.12514.

Ibarra, I. (2003) *Working Identity: Unconventional Strategies for Reinventing Your Career*. Boston, MA: Harvard Business School Press.

Lawson, C. and Lopes-Bento, C. (2024) 'Miss or match? The impact of PhD training on job market satisfaction,' *Research Policy*, 53(3), 104945. doi: 10.1016/j.respol.2023.104945.

Li, H. and Horta, H. (2024). 'Exploring the identity development of PhD graduates transitioning to non-researcher roles.' *Higher Education Quarterly*, 78, pp. 421–435. doi: 10.1111/hequ.12452.

McKenzie, L. (2021) 'Unequal expressions: emotions and narratives of leaving and remaining in precarious academia,' *Social Anthropology*, 29, pp. 527–542. doi: 10.1111/1469-8676.13011.

Sauermann, H. and Roach, M. (2012) 'Science PhD career preferences: levels, changes, and advisor encouragement,' *PLoS ONE*, 7(5), e36307. doi: 10.1371/journal.pone.0036307.

Spronken-Smith, R., Brown, K. and Cameron, C. (2024) 'Work happiness of PhD graduates across different employment sectors,' *New Zealand Journal of Educational Studies*, 59, pp. 565–582. doi: 10.1007/s40841-024-00339-1.

Zimmerman, A.M. (2018) 'Navigating the path to a biomedical science career,' *PLoS ONE*, 13(9), e0203783. doi: 10.1371/journal.pone.0203783.

2 Getting started on your transition beyond academia

Once you've devised your support statement and feel ready to explore possible futures beyond academia, the natural next question might be *where to start.* This is where many researchers head straight to a search engine or large job board, stick in search terms such as 'PhD psychology jobs,' 'researcher jobs,' and hope for the best. Starting out like this, however, is limiting for several reasons, including:

- Even when they are looking for high-level research skills, up to 80% of employers do not explicitly ask for a doctorate or postdoc in a specific subject area (Mewburn et al., 2020). Searching according to your qualification level and academic discipline may therefore miss some opportunities in line with your skills and interests.
- It's difficult to guess useful search terms when you're not clear what you're looking for.
- Your search results will be limited to roles advertised at that time and are unlikely to be fully representative of your options.
- Results gained from such searches can appear random, irrelevant, or overwhelming.

DOI: 10.4324/9781003589785-3

For others, 'getting started' means devising a 'plan' or deciding on a career 'path.' For many reasons, I use the words 'plan' or 'path' with caution, as they imply a linearity which rarely reflects the trajectory of real-life careers. Instead, I prefer the following quote often attributed to British businessman Sir Dominic Cadbury:

> There is no such thing as a career path. It's crazy paving and you have to lay it yourself.

To unpack this idea, and understand effective ways to get started exploring what's out there for you beyond academia, let's look at some key ideas from the field of career theory to offer some suggestions.

What's the evidence?

When I began studying for my career guidance qualification, I was delighted to discover that career development is its own academic discipline, drawing on fields including psychology, sociology, and cultural studies, many of which I was familiar with from my humanities doctorate. As the discipline continues to evolve, theories of career choice that assume our career decisions are rational and that prioritise the formulation of linear plans, have come under criticism (e.g. Bright and Pryor, 2019; Mitchell et al., 1999), with some contemporary theorists arguing that rather than being pesky problems to solve, we ought to embrace messiness, chance, and uncertainty as essential aspects of our careers. In this respect, a career is not something that results from a one-off decision; it is a lifelong process of learning, re-learning, and adapting your work and skills in the context of fast-changing job markets and working environments. And when evidence shows that researchers from disadvantaged backgrounds, who are carers, who work multiple jobs, or who start their education later are more likely to have nonlinear trajectories, appreciating the messy reality of careers is crucial (Vlasits et al., 2023).

The Chaos Theory of Careers (CTC) argues that the notion of 'career planning' greatly oversimplifies the complexity of human beings, since the realities of 'complexity, change, connection, and chance' mean that we often cannot predict the outcomes of our plans (Bright and Pryor, 2019: 5). Similarly, a school of career theory known as 'planned happenstance' questions the role of certainty and planning in career development, arguing that long-term career plans can be problematic, especially given that the future of work is increasingly uncertain, and both our personal priorities and the labour market are ever-changing (e.g. Krumboltz, 1998). Instead of focusing on plans to direct your career, the planned happenstance approach would encourage you to focus on learning how to capitalise on *unplanned* events, and work on initiating situations that can increase your chances of finding opportunities. Despite being popularised back in the late 1990s, the key principles of planned happenstance continue to be hailed as profoundly relevant today, 'in a professional landscape characterized by constant change and complexity' which demands 'continuous development of adaptive skills, the cultivation of a strong and diverse network, and a reflective mindset that learns from every outcome' (Adha et al., 2025: 223).

Such theories reflect the idea that in real life, many careers emerge through a complex web of chance events, adaptation to shifting circumstances, and making your own luck. A recent example of this is the concept of the 'Squiggly Career' (Tupper and Ellis, 2020) which argues that whilst career plans may have worked in a job market 'where you could envisage the future with a high degree of certainty,' they just don't cut it in our current climate, at least in the Global North (131). Consequently, 'squiggly career' thinking encourages shifting focus from career 'plans,' and instead viewing your career as a journey on which you continually learn what you're good at, what matters to you in your work, and explore different places where these things can be put to good use.

Research in the field of career development shows this 'squiggliness' of real-life careers at work. For example, a study of university students and graduates in the UK showed that whilst students tended to view their next career steps as a 'heavy decision' that 'will likely influence the rest of my life' (Houston and Cunningham, 2018: 27), graduates' stories presented a different picture. Once in work, the graduates talked about learning from jobs they didn't enjoy, experiencing a lack of fulfilment in what they expected to be their dream job, and using these experiences to better understand their preferences and devise their next moves accordingly (29). Whereas the students in the study approached choosing their first graduate job as an irrevocable decision to choose a defined 'path,' the graduates' stories instead suggested that for many of us, a career is an *incremental process* in which we learn from our experiences and take steps to 'tweak' our professional activities in ways that allow us to do more of what we want to do, and less of what we don't.

Looking specifically at doctoral graduates moving beyond academia, a study by McAlpine and Amundsen (2016) found similar examples of such incremental career 'tweaking.' For one participant, 'happenstance' played a key role in her career move into sustainability: after taking up a short-term academic position, she missed working outdoors as she had during some volunteering experience alongside her doctorate (82–83). Another participant who aspired to an academic career landed an academic research position post-PhD, but later moved into a role in a private foundation as this allowed him to keep undertaking research and to follow his interests in social justice, but to lose what he described as the 'all-encompassing' nature of academic life (76). As in the previous study, these people didn't create a plan, choose a path, execute it, and then stop. Rather, the jobs they moved into were first steps, not final destinations: steps from which they learned more about what they wanted from their work, and then used this learning to inform their next moves.

Indeed, evidence also shows that increasing numbers of researchers also 'squiggle' their careers between academia and other sectors. For example, analysis of the LinkedIn profiles of over 21,000 higher education researchers in the UK showed that around 36% had previously held positions in at least one other sector (Ospina and Rodriguez, 2023: 2), whilst a survey of researchers working in the EU revealed that, on average, 24.8% had previously worked in the private sector (5). This suggests that either completely 'staying in' or 'leaving' academia may not be your only choices, as many researchers appear to build multi-sectoral careers which challenge the binary between 'academic' and 'non-academic' routes.

What does this mean for you?

Rethinking a career as something other than a linear path can be exciting or jarring, depending on your outlook and experience. If you've come 'straight through' an educational system where completion of one level apparently 'unlocks' the next, like an academic version of Super Mario, the idea of a 'squiggly career' may feel somewhat alien. Completing your doctorate may 'unlock' access to postdoc work, but this certainly isn't the case for everyone. And for those who do progress to postdoctoral research or teaching, there are certainly no guarantees that this will then 'unlock' a permanent academic position. This is why approaching the end of your doctorate or postdoc may feel like standing on the brink of an abyss: you have reached a point where there is no 'natural next step' left, and it's now up to you to work out where to go next. And whilst this can be daunting, for some researchers it can also feel liberating.

The good news is that the evidence examined above suggests that not having a detailed 'plan' for your next steps doesn't necessarily give reason to panic. Whilst we all have differing levels of comfort with the unknown, scholarship suggests that not having things 'all figured out' is fine; in fact, some career theorists might even call it sensible. But if a carefully curated, linear path or plan isn't what we need to get started... then what is?

Above, we saw examples of individuals shaping their career journeys by tweaking what they do as they go, rather than making one-off, irrevocable career decisions. Some knew that there were things they wanted to *keep* doing in their next roles, like to keep using certain skills and pursuing specific interests. Some knew that there were things they wanted to *lose* from their current work, like the way in which academia blurred boundaries between their work and personal lives. Finally, all of them seemed to identify things that they wanted their next jobs to *add* to their professional lives which they didn't currently have: a greater sense of fulfilment; more time spent outdoors; or better work-life balance. Getting started with exploring careers beyond academia therefore becomes less about answering the question 'what do I want to do with the rest of my life?' and more about working out 'how could I tweak what I'm doing now to bring it more in line with what matters to me?' Herminia Ibarra captures this in her description of career change as a process of 'figuring out how to transfer old preferences and values to new and different contexts, and how to integrate those with changing priorities' (2003: 163). A useful way to get started, therefore, is by identifying what you would like to take with you into your next work, and what aspects of your work you would like to change.

A simple framework to help with this is to ask yourself the following:

If I were to turn what I'm doing now (doctorate, post-doc, academic job, etc.) into my ideal job:

- *What aspects of it would I want to* ***keep?***
- *What aspects of it would I want to* ***lose?***
- *What aspects would I want to* ***add*** *to it that I don't have at the moment?*

I call this working out your **'Keep/lose/add'** profile.

Examples of the types of 'aspects' that you might like to keep, lose, or add include:

- Work activities, i.e. the things that you do every day in your work.
- Your working environment, e.g. setting and location.
- Working culture, e.g. supportive, team-based, collaborative, fast-paced, etc.
- How the work fits your personal circumstances and needs like work-life balance, salary, adjustments for health conditions and disabilities, and so on.

Working out what you most want your next career step to help you to keep, lose, and add is useful for several reasons. Firstly, it helps you to view your career as an incremental process of 'tweaking' your work, rather than pressuring yourself to get your career transition 'right first time.' Secondly, it lets you focus on how you want your work to fit in with the rest of your life. And thirdly, it can help you to work out whether you can achieve your desired 'tweaks' within your current role or workplace, or whether you need to jump ship.

Once you start to explore your options, your keep/ lose /add profile will be a useful guide for what you want to know about certain options, and what to ask people during your networking to find this out. When you come to apply and interview for roles beyond academia, your keep/lose/add profile can also help you to construct a convincing narrative as to how the roles you are targeting fit with your motivations and goals.

Get to work

Exercise 2.1: Your keep/lose/add profile

Now it's time for you to complete your keep/lose/add profile. Use an outline like Table 2.1 to record how you would change your current or previous work into your ideal work. As an example, Table 2.1 shows how I would have answered this towards the end of my doctorate. Based on my answers, it's no surprise that I ended up working in career guidance and training!

Table 2.1 Compiling your 'keep/lose/add' profile

Keep	*Lose*	*Add*
Teaching or advising in some capacity	Working on something esoteric that I struggle to explain to my family	Seeing the impact of my work more quickly than in academia, where it can take years for a piece of work to get published
Using presenting and public speaking skills	Working on my own most of the time	More interaction with a variety of people in my daily work
Creating materials and resources, preferably educational		The opportunity to work with people on a 1:1 basis rather than just teaching groups
Feeling like I'm always learning		Greater separation between 'work time' and 'down time'

Once you've completed your keep/lose/add profile, consider the following:

- How do you feel about your answers? Do any surprise you?
- If you have next career steps in mind, how likely are these to align with your profile? If you don't know, how can you find this out?
- What are your non-negotiables? It's unlikely that you'll be able to achieve everything in your keep/lose/add

profile with your first job beyond academia. If you had to choose one thing to lose first and one thing to add first, what would these be?

- Do you see any potential tensions? For example, you may have things that predominantly happen in academia (such as teaching a very niche subject) in your 'keep' column, but also have things characteristic of academia in your country (such as precarious work and having to bid for funding) in your 'lose' column. If this is the case, what compromises might you need to make?

Once you have created your profile, consider your 'keep' column and ask yourself *what it is* that you enjoy about the things you have listed. It can be easy to jump to conclusions: for example, if you've listed teaching in your 'keep' column, you might assume that becoming a teacher or a lecturer are your most intuitive options. However, identifying *why* you enjoy the things that you enjoy can help you to generate less obvious career ideas that might give you a similar sense of satisfaction. The next three sections offer tips on this, specifically if you listed teaching, research, and/or public engagement in your 'keep' column. They also contain examples that challenge the dichotomy of 'staying in' or 'leaving' academia, including combining other-sector work with teaching or research, or by undertaking 'academic adjacent' roles connected to areas such as pedagogy, research culture, or student support.

'Keeping' teaching

If you listed 'teaching' as something you'd like to 'keep,' consider *what it is about teaching* that you enjoy. The answer could reveal some themes that might help you to broaden your options. Below are some examples:

You want to 'keep' teaching because you love your subject and want to inspire other people to enjoy it too.

If this is the case, then teaching your subject might seem like an obvious option. However, you might also want to consider:

- Exploring roles and opportunities with other types of organisations that advocate for, and encourage engagement with, specific subject areas: for example, professional bodies and learned societies.
- Whether education linked to your subject area takes place in other settings beyond the traditional classroom, for example in community organisations, museums, galleries, charities, private sector companies, and so on.
- Negotiating time to stay involved in teaching with your potential employer(s). Moving away from full-time academic employment may not necessarily mean that you have to give up teaching completely, depending on your new role and employer.

You want to 'keep' teaching because you enjoy simplifying complex information into something that people can understand.

If this is the case, then you could think about:

- Policy-based roles in which you develop expertise in a particular area, advise on this area, and synthesise information into easily digestible briefings for stakeholders, decision-makers, and so on.
- Industry roles like Technical Communications or Scientific Adviser, which involve translating technical and

scientific aspects of products into claims that consumers can understand.
- Roles in which you help customers to understand how to use a technical device, drug, or other product, like Field Applications or Medical Science Liaison.

You want to 'keep' teaching because you enjoy helping and supporting students.

If this sounds like you, then depending on your experience it may be worth considering student-facing work such as:

- Academic skills support.
- Training and development roles in higher education, such as researcher development.
- Other support roles that may need separate professional qualifications in some countries, such as career guidance or student welfare.
- Exploring opportunities with future employers to get involved in university outreach activity. One example of this is a doctoral graduate who was given time by his employer (a life science consulting firm) to manage an internship programme for doctoral researchers, including training incoming interns.

'Keeping' research

If you listed 'research' as something you'd like to 'keep,' reflect on what it is that you enjoy most about research. This could give you clues about types of work that will let you use your researcher brain in the ways you most prefer. Below are some examples:

You want to 'keep' research because you're driven by the idea of contributing to a particular field.

A full-time academic job may not be the only role in which you work towards this goal. You could also:

- Research companies and organisations that create products, services, and knowledge linked your preferred field, for example, charities that address child exploitation, think tanks focused on social justice, or companies that develop technologies or drugs to treat certain conditions more effectively. These could be potential future employers.
- Approach start-ups (new companies in the early stages of development) whose products and services link with your area of interest. You could identify these through online searches for incubators, accelerators, or science parks in your location, or by searching for companies that have recently received investment. 'Recent seed raises in <X country>' is one search term you could use.
- Explore opportunities to keep up your research 'on the side' as an independent researcher. See Tania's case study below for tips on this.

You want to 'keep' research because you enjoy using your research skills and techniques, but don't mind – or actively prefer – applying them to a different field from your doctoral/postdoc work.

If this is the case, remember that research-based jobs exist in many different settings. Options you could explore include:

- Research-based roles in the public sector, including central and local government.

- Roles with research agencies or consultancies, where you will undertake research for a range of different clients.
- Roles in clinical or patient-centred outcomes research, especially if you've enjoyed working with participants.
- Research and development roles (e.g. Research Scientist) that use your existing research skills or lab techniques but apply them to a different area or goal.
- Moving into a field of work with its own theoretical grounding and body of scholarship, as I mentioned earlier in reference to career guidance. Examples include pedagogy, librarianship and information studies, and educational management. If there is an area of work that you are interested in, search online to see if there are any journals associated with it. If there are, this indicates academic activity in this area to which you could ultimately contribute.

'Keeping' public engagement

If 'public engagement,' 'outreach,' 'research communication' or something similar features in your 'keep' column, consider what it is about this type of activity that motivates you. Depending on your level of experience, this could link to a range of next steps, for example:

You want to 'keep' public engagement and outreach because you feel strongly about access to education and social mobility.

- Research charities or other organisations in your commutable area which are focused on these missions. Working for such an organisation could be one way of aligning your work with your values.

- Research activities undertaken by your university or institute, and others in your area, to engage with schools. This could be a way to gain experience for a role in outreach, widening participation, schools' liaison, or whatever this type of activity may be called in your country or region.

You want to 'keep' public engagement and outreach because you enjoy communicating research to others, especially to non-specialists.

- Research organisations that not only undertake research, but who fund research and thus need to communicate that research to wider audiences, be it patients, the public, young people, government and policy makers, etc.
- This type of work might be done by research communications professionals in a variety of settings including universities, charities, research or scientific facilities, research funders, professional bodies or learned societies.

Case study

The case studies in this section show real-life examples of how a range of people from different academic backgrounds have managed to 'keep' – or even add more of – what they enjoyed in academia in their new careers. These are just some illustrations of how moving beyond 'traditional' academic research and teaching roles doesn't mean completely giving up your identity as an academic or a researcher. In fact, you may even be able to find a better balance of what you are looking for professionally by looking beyond the academy.

Case study 2.1 Tania's story – keeping up research 'on the side'

Tania is a historian of the Medical Humanities with an academic background in art history and visual culture. She now works as a Research Development Manager in a UK university but continues with her academic research in her own time. We heard about Tania's career transition in Chapter 1, but here she specifically discusses the possibilities for 'keeping' academic research as part of your professional mix, alongside other-sector work. She says:

'Twice I've had the opportunity to take up academic posts; I've now chosen a different option, but I remain passionate about my research and finding creative ways to keep integrating it in my everyday life. As well as more "typical" academic funding schemes such as postdoctoral or early career fellowships, there are grant schemes open to people who are not on research or teaching contracts, and even to independent scholars. They are not easy to spot, but some options to consider if you are interested in going down this route include:

- Exploring discipline-specific associations (which may require paid membership). The small grants that have recently funded my research as an independent scholar have been through these associations. They also run annual conferences to help you disseminate your research and network with your academic community. They might even offer bursaries to offset those attendance costs, as the definition of "early career researcher" is becoming more diverse and inclusive of people in a range of circumstances.

- Libraries may offer funding for short stays to use collections, especially those with specialised holdings.
- Investigate opportunities for small research grants (SRGs). Some funding bodies (such as the British Academy, in partnership with the Leverhulme Trust in the UK) offer small research grants which are open to independent scholars.
- Involvement with other researchers' funded projects. You may already know academics working on topics in your area and could, through networking, offer to collaborate with them. You could act as a researcher on another academic's grant which, depending on the time required, may mean negotiating an arrangement with your main employer (e.g. releasing you for one day a week for you to spend on research).
- Gaining honorary researcher status (unpaid). Some institutions are open to offering this, which usually provides library access and maybe even an institutional email address. This can help you to retain affiliation to an institution with specialisms in one's field (e.g. a research centre). However, the process may not be straightforward: deferential enquiry is likely required via an academic contact to find out about the internal process.'

Case study 2.2 Carlos's story – focusing on research in industry

Carlos did his undergraduate and Master's degrees and his PhD in Industrial Engineering and Production in Spain. Here, he discusses how shifting his career beyond academia helped him to 'keep' a focus on research:

'After my PhD, I continued to teach and research back to my former university in Spain. However, I wanted to dedicate more time to doing research than my academic position would allow, so I turned to industry. I joined IBM in the UK initially as a Postdoctoral Research Scientist and later got promoted to Research Staff member.

When I applied for the Postdoctoral Research Scientist role, it was only after the interview that I realised how closely linked to my research the opportunity was. Undertaking a postdoc in industry gave me a good balance of research and its practical application; I presented some of my work at a couple of conferences and published three papers, two in Physics of Fluids and one in Future Generation Computer Systems. I also had a first author patent issued. In fact, the journals I published in once I moved into industry were even more relevant to my background and interests than the ones I published in during my time at the university! In large tech companies there are many experts from different disciplines working together towards shared goals, meaning there are opportunities to undertake research that is applicable to both industries and to wider society.'

Case study 2.3 Showforth's story – shifting academic skills into freelancing

Showforth studied Microbiology at Bachelor's and Master's level in Nigeria, before undertaking a PhD in Ireland followed by two Research Fellow contracts. After just less than a year in a researcher development role in a UK university, he resigned and relocated to Ghana. Here, he outlines how he has managed to keep applying a range of his academic-related skills and expertise in his current freelance work:

'My career transition is still very much a work in progress. However, I have decided to leverage my mixture of skills, knowledge, and experience to start building a freelance consulting career whilst exploring other longer-term options in Ghana. So far, I have drawn on:

- My knowledge and skills in journal reviewing and editing to run workshops for researchers and students on topics including identifying research gaps, academic writing, and reviewing literature.
- My research and writing skills, which I used to secure a short-term consultancy role as a scientific content creator with an international research-for-development organisation.
- My understanding of the European funding landscape that I developed through my time as an Expert Evaluator for the European Commission, which has led to some potential collaborations.

- My passion for microbiology, which I use as a Visiting Senior Lecturer at a university in Nigeria, and also to visit schools to introduce this fascinating subject to students.

I am still exploring roles in other sectors such as international research organisations, academic exchange organisations, university associations, and embassies. So far, however, the skills, knowledge, and experience that I developed during my time in academia have helped me to create opportunities and networks for myself that I can call on to further develop my career.'

Case study 2.4 Emma's story – keeping alive a love of science communication

Emma currently works as a Product Lead for a medical device company. Her first job after her PhD was as a Field Application Specialist for a scientific instrument company. Here, she discusses how her industry career so far has allowed her to keep applying the public engagement skills she enjoyed using during her doctorate:

'Throughout my PhD, I really enjoyed getting involved in outreach activities such as hosting a microscopy stand at a local science museum during school holidays and talking about my research at a public library. I was also privileged enough to speak about my research on a podcast and on a local radio show, both of which I liked because they involved communicating science in an accessible way.

All the industry roles I've had so far have involved putting these public engagement and science communication skills to good use. For example, a lot of my work has involved talking to key opinion leaders, healthcare professionals, and scientific researchers across multiple disciplines, working with them to communicate their feedback to support the development of various products, with the aim to ultimately help improve scientific and patient outcomes. In my current Product Lead role, one of the things I enjoy most is pulling together stakeholders from across the company to make sure that we develop and launch products that satisfy our customers' needs. It was through my experience of communicating research to a variety of audiences during my PhD that I honed the skills needed to be understood by a range of colleagues with varying levels of scientific knowledge. If you want to keep using these kinds of skills in your career, remember that research communication and public engagement aren't your only options, and that many roles in scientific and healthcare companies, like the ones I've held in marketing, let you use these skills, too.'

Takeaways

- Searching job boards, or trying to devise a rigid career plan, are often limiting ways to start exploring career options in a complex job market.

- Traditional linear notions of career 'pathways' and 'plans' do not reflect the unpredictable nature of modern careers and labour markets.
- Contemporary career theories instead encourage us to embrace uncertainty, chance, and adaptability in career development rather than focusing on detailed planning.
- Research suggests that many professionals, including doctorate holders, build their careers through incremental adjustments ('tweaking'), learning from their experiences and adapting to changing circumstances rather than following rigid plans or making 'one-off' career decisions.
- Identifying which aspects of your current work you would most like to keep and most like to change can therefore be a useful way to get started on thinking about your next steps and moving towards these.
- Reflecting on *why* you enjoy what you do in your current work can help you to move away from 'obvious' career ideas and open up to broader options.
- 'Staying in academia' and 'leaving academia' aren't the only options: many former doctoral and postdoctoral researchers combine other-sector work with teaching or research, or work in 'academic adjacent' roles that keep them connected to academia.

References

Adha, I., Afdal, A. and Hariko, R. (2025) 'Implementation of planned happenstance in career planning and decision making,' *Widyagogik*, 13(3), pp. 209–224.

Bright, J.E.H. and Pryor, R.G.L. (2019) 'The chaos theory of careers: emerging from simplification to complexity, certainty to uncertainty,' *Asia Pacific Career Development Journal*, 2(1), pp. 1–15. Available at: https://asiapacificcda.org/Resources/APCDJ/A0002_1_001.pdf [Accessed 20 March 2025].

Houston, K. and Cunningham, E. (2018) 'Waiting for a career epiphany – a barrier to career decision-making?' *Journal of the National Institute for Career Education and Counselling*, 40, pp. 25–32. doi: 10.20856/jnicec.4005.

Ibarra, I. (2003) *Working Identity: Unconventional Strategies for Reinventing Your Career*. Boston, MA: Harvard Business School Press.

Krumboltz, J.D. (1998) 'Serendipity is not serendipitous,' *Journal of Counseling Psychology*, 45(4), pp. 390–392. doi: 10.1037/0022-0167.45.4.390.

McAlpine, L. and Amundsen, C. (2016) *Post-PhD Career Trajectories: Intentions, Decision-Making and Life Aspirations*. London: Palgrave Pivot.

Mewburn, I., Grant, W.J., Suominen, H. and Kizimchuk, S. (2020) 'A machine learning analysis of the non-academic employment opportunities for Ph.D. graduates in Australia,' *Higher Education Policy,* 33, pp. 799–813. doi: 10.1057/s41307-018-0098-4

Mitchell, K.E., Levin, S.A. and Krumboltz, J.D. (1999) 'Planned happenstance: constructing unexpected career opportunities,' *Journal of Counseling & Development*, 77, pp. 115–124. doi: 10.1002/j.1556-6676.1999.tb02431.x.

Ospina, J.V. and Rodriguez, M. (2023) *Quantitative report: Building a data-driven picture of researcher intersectoral mobility in the UK*. London: National Centre for Universities and Business. Available at: https://www.ncub.co.uk/insight/building-a-data-driven-picture-of-researcher-intersectoral-mobility-in-the-uk/ [Accessed 14 April 2025].

Tupper, H. and Ellis, S. (2020) *The Squiggly Career*. London: Penguin.

Vlasits, A.L., Smith, M.L., Maldonado, M. and Brixius-Anderko, S (2023) 'Supporting nonlinear careers to diversify science,' *PLoS Biology,* 21(9). doi: 10.1371/journal.pbio.3002291

3 Applying your skills beyond academia

You've spent some time identifying your priorities for your next career steps, so now it's time to start devising career ideas that align with these, and that make good use of your skills. However, when you're surrounded by other researchers who are good at the same things you are, it's so easy to take your skills for granted: especially in an academic culture so based on critique. To manage a career transition beyond academia, you need to both understand the value that you can bring to potential employers, and to *believe* in that value. To help with this, let's look at what the evidence says about how skills developed in academia are applicable to other sectors.

What's the evidence?

When we discuss articulating your skills effectively in Chapter 6, we will highlight some of the key challenges around how doctoral and postdoctoral researchers' skills are perceived beyond academia. The job in hand for now, however, is to unravel what doctoral and postdoctoral skills really are and how you can apply them to different settings.

DOI: 10.4324/9781003589785-4

The good news is that evidence suggests the skills gained through academic research are highly applicable beyond academia. For example, studies show that even if a doctorate was not a requirement for their role, doctoral graduates and former postdocs working beyond academia:

- Agree that 'transferable skills' gained during the PhD 'were essential for both acquiring and working in their current role' (Boyd and McAlinden, 2016: 5).
- Feel that much of the day-to-day experience gained from academic research 'is needed in many different roles' beyond academia (Peacey and Romijn, 2026: 6).
- Feel that managing research alongside personal commitments left them 'more self-sufficient, multi-functional, and especially good at time management' (Pham, 2025: 440).

Evidence shows that skills gained through academic research are valued by a range of employers, though as a recent systematic review highlights, up-to-date literature covering employers' perceptions of researchers is extremely limited (Muurlink et al., 2024: 959). Amongst the little there is, however, one study of 96 employers of doctoral graduates found that three-quarters claimed that losing their doctoral-qualified employees would have 'either a business critical or a significant impact on operations' (Diamond *et al.,* 2014: 4), whilst 73% of UK employers surveyed in another study said that they would welcome more applications from doctoral graduates (Rubio and Hooley, 2010: 2). Of course, the specific skills valued beyond academia depend on a range of factors, including the employer, sector, and role(s) in question. For example, moving into a non-technical role means that 'general analytical skills, project management skills and problem-solving capability' are most likely to be applicable to your job, whilst working in academia or public research is more likely to require knowledge from your academic research area (Lee et al., 2010: 877). If we look closely at some of these studies, then, we can start to piece together the main types of knowledge and skills that you possess as a researcher, and that you can leverage in your transition from academia to other sectors.

The most obvious of these is subject-specialist knowledge, with 86% of employers agreeing that they value this when recruiting staff with a doctorate (CIHE, 2010: 7). This seems particularly relevant to research and development roles in industry, in which specialist knowledge can be 'applied quickly in the business,' and employers value candidates who are up to date on scientific literature and developments (9). Beyond subject knowledge, skills in using specific technical equipment or techniques that are directly relevant to a company's products and processes are also valued (CIHE, 2010: 7).

As well as subject knowledge and technical ability, several studies also highlight the transferability of broader research skills. In the research referred to above, 87% of employers surveyed agreed that they valued the research skills that doctoral graduates brought to their organisations (CIHE, 2010: 7). This is by no means limited to STEM disciplines, with employers citing social science research skills and general abilities to conduct, evaluate, and interpret research as valuable for 'research and research management posts in social and market research, industry and commerce.' (Elias et al., 2005: 6), as well as particular demand for quantitative and statistical research skills (71). Furthermore, data analysis also ranks highly as a skill (or set of skills) that employers especially value in doctoral graduates (Rubio and Hooley, 2010: 2).

Beyond subject knowledge, technical expertise, research skills, and data analysis are the broader skills that you gain from academic research. Of these, employers report finding particular value in skills including 'problem-solving, quick learning, efficient assimilation of information, maturity of thought, and attention to detail' (McAlpine and Inouye, 2022: 1658), as well as 'abstract cognitive skills, including critical thinking and argument construction' (Bryan and Guccione, 2018: 1129). Furthermore, having staff with doctoral-level qualifications can also help companies to build credibility with clients and to distinguish themselves from competitors (McAlpine and Inouye, 2022: 1658).

Finally, another transferable skillset derived from academic research is the ability to navigate the ways in which universities and academia work. This skillset involves 'knowledge of academic attitudes' and 'insights into the operations of universities' gained from experience within academia, which can translate particularly well into roles within academic administration or student support (Guerin, 2020: 317–318), or roles that 'facilitate engagement between universities and industry' (320).

Whilst research is encouraging about the transferability of skills developed in academia, this transferability may differ according to your subject background. For example, whilst the proportion of STEM doctorate holders employed in sectors beyond academia 'suggests clear demand for scientific research skills in the wider economy,' the equivalent demand for skills gained from social sciences and humanities research 'is less certain' (Hancock, 2021: 529), with individuals from research backgrounds in the humanities and social sciences less likely to be in roles that require doctoral-level qualifications and skills (Paolo and Mañé, 2016: 439). However, whilst subject knowledge and technical skills from most STEM disciplines may appear more directly applicable to other sectors, researchers from the arts, humanities, and social sciences are especially well placed to demonstrate skills key to the modern knowledge economy such as persuasion, emotional intelligence, and teaching others: skills which, in the near future, the World Economic Forum predict will be in higher demand than technical skills like programming which have clear shelf-lives (Guerin, 2020: 320).

What does this mean for you?

The literature reviewed above highlights how doctoral and postdoctoral research equips you with a rich set of skills and experiences that are in demand in other sectors, suggesting **six key types** of knowledge or skill that are especially valued beyond academia:

- Subject-specific knowledge.
- Research skills and methods.
- Technical ability, including skills in using specialist equipment and technologies.
- Data analysis skills.
- Broader 'transferable' skills.
- Skills in navigating how research and universities work.

Breaking down your own academic experience into these six skill areas can help you to see how your own skills might map across to a range of potential next steps. We've also seen how this is even more important if you come from the social sciences, humanities, and less-applied subjects, where connections between previous research experience and demand within wider labour markets may be less 'obvious.'

Let's now look at each of these six types of knowledge and skills in more detail to help you apply this framework to your own situation. Of course, just because you *can* transfer your skills across to something doesn't mean that you have to; this is why your 'keep/lose/add' profile from Chapter 2 is useful in helping you to understand which skills you most want to use in your next role.

Subject-specific knowledge

Obvious employers who will be interested in your subject-specific knowledge are academic departments, research groups, and labs. However, other types of organisations might also be on the lookout for someone with your specialist expertise. For example, if your research examined the behaviour of aluminium alloys under stress, and there's a company who needs that expertise to make sure their aircraft components can withstand the necessary pressures, then they could be a potential future employer. Similarly, if your research has compared war memorialisation practices in the UK and France, and a heritage organisation needs someone to advise on how to manage memorials with contested heritage, that's another example of transferring subject knowledge into another sector.

If using your subject knowledge features in the 'keep' column of your keep/lose/add profile, one way to identify potential employers is by researching which industries and organisations are working on practical applications linked to your specialist knowledge. As the example of war memorialisation above shows, this isn't always exclusive to STEM researchers. You could also explore what kinds of organisations work to increase awareness of, or access to, your subject area. These might include learned societies or membership associations, of which you may already be a member (e.g. Royal Society of Chemistry, American Association for the Advancement of Science, Historical Association, and so on). If you aren't already aware of such organisations linked to your subject area, search online for 'membership association [biology/ history/ psychology etc.].' Once you identify an example, find the organisation's LinkedIn page (if they have one) and select the 'people' tab to see what kinds of roles people do there and if any of these could be potential options for you.

As we saw above, however, a role doesn't have to identically match the subject matter of your research for you to be a good candidate. Sometimes, your more general subject knowledge can also be transferred to roles beyond academia. For example, a medical communications agency hiring for a trainee medical writer might generally ask that candidates have a 'strong life sciences background' rather than specifying knowledge of particular diseases or therapeutic areas. You are by no means restricted to roles connected to your current specialism; there may also be opportunities for you to leverage your more general subject knowledge – plus enthusiasm for the role in question – to move into another sector.

Research skills and methods

If subject expertise is *what* you research, your broader research skills describe how you do your research: your methodology. Unless you've been working on something extremely niche, chances are that the methods you have used to undertake your research can be applied to other fields. Examples of such methods and skills include:

- Literature reviewing
- Wet lab skills
- Testing techniques
- Modelling and simulation methods
- Interviewing and focus groups
- Survey design
- Archival research
- Participant-based research with specific populations
- Using AI tools responsibly and transparently within your research field

If using your research skills featured in the 'keep' column of your 'keep/lose/add' profile, then considering which types of employers might value these skills is a way of exploring potential options. An example of this kind of transferability would be a doctoral graduate from psychology who now uses semi-structured interviewing skills in a patient outcomes research role for a healthcare consultancy, which involves recruiting and interviewing patients in clinical trials about their experiences of treatments.

If you have a background in the humanities, however, you may not immediately relate to the term 'research skills,' or 'techniques.' For my own doctorate in English Literature, for example, I'd struggle to articulate a specific methodology or any qualitative or quantitative techniques: on the face of it, I just read books. On reflection, however, there was still a method to how I chose, analysed, and used those books. I used targeted searches to identify relevant literature. I analysed that literature to see how the representation of something had changed over time.

I then used that information to form an evidence-based conclusion. The same goes for you if your research has focused on analysing items such as literary texts, works of art, musical scores, and so on: whatever your sources or subject matter, you are experienced in this broader research process which is transferable to other settings.

To explore options beyond academia that use your research skills, an alumni search to see what other people with these skills have gone on to do can help you to generate ideas. Using a browser rather than the mobile app, find your current or former university's page on LinkedIn and from the menu across the middle select 'Alumni.' This will show a range of categories you can use to filter alumni. Scroll across to the 'what they are skilled at' filter and use 'add' to type in a skill that you'd like to keep using in your future work. This usually works better if you are specific, e.g. entering 'focus groups' or 'mass spectrometry' rather than 'research skills.' Looking at the profiles of the people in your search results can help to identify potential employers who value these skills, and the titles of potential roles that involve using these skills. Typing 'PhD' or similar into the alumni search bar could further filter results to people who are qualified to doctoral level.

Skills in using specialist equipment and technologies

During your research, you may also have used specific technical equipment, instruments, materials, or other similar products, and hence have become an experienced user of these. This could involve anything from lab consumables, microscopes, scanners, types of scientific software, and so on; ultimately, anything that your lab, research group, or you as an individual have to 'buy in' or acquire in order to complete your research.

Your experience of using such equipment and materials could be of significant value in industry, including to the companies who produce and sell them. These companies will not only employ people who make the products; they will also employ teams to help them to improve their products and to develop new ones (like Emma's role in case study 2.4 in Chapter 2), to train customers in how to use these products, to understand how their products are used *in situ*, and to market and sell the products. All these functions could offer potential avenues of future employment beyond academia. One example of this is a former post-doc who discovered her new career in technical sales for a protein development and manufacturing company through chatting to a sales rep who visited her lab.

To explore such potential options, start by looking up on LinkedIn the companies who make the products you use in your research. Go to the 'people' tab (as we mentioned earlier with regards to memberships associations) to see what kinds of roles people have there. You could even narrow it down by typing 'PhD,' 'EngD' or similar into the search bar within this section, to see which roles are done by doctorate holders. Also, take opportunities to talk to people from organisations such as biotech companies, lab equipment manufacturers, and other similar organisations at conferences and exhibitions, or even when they visit your own labs or departments.

Data analysis skills

Whilst research skills, technical skills, and data analysis skills have significant crossover, here we're using 'data analysis' to refer to the skills you've gained specifically through processing and analysing your data. This could include using coding languages for example, or any other analytical methods that could transfer to topics or problems beyond your research area. If you've taught yourself these techniques then you can easily pick up new ones: you may not always need lots of experience with one specific package or coding language to prove that you're capable of a particular role. An example of leveraging data analysis skills is a doctoral graduate who went on to apply the statistical data analysis and coding skills gained from studying the decay of subatomic particles to a data scientist role in the transport industry, working on problems like the traffic impact of building a new road.

Importantly, analytical skills aren't limited to quantitative data analysis. If you work in the arts or humanities, for example, you may not feel that you deal with data at all. However, if you've spent time analysing what participants say in interviews, analysing literary texts to identify how something is represented, or analysing musical scores to identify similarities, then these are all useful examples of your analytical ability: namely, your ability to spot complex connections and trends and to use these to answer a question, form an argument, or solve a problem.

Broader 'transferable' skills

Beyond the skills gained through what you research, how you conduct your research, and how you analyse your 'data,' are the myriad other abilities you will have developed through completing doctoral or postdoctoral research. Call them broader skills, 'soft' skills, personal skills, whatever you like... they're what's left if you take away anything specific to your research topic, subject area, or methodology.

In the studies reviewed above, just a few of the broader skills that employers cited as valuable to their companies, or that participants reported as useful in their current roles, were:

- Problem-solving
- Quick learning/efficient assimilation of information
- Attention to detail
- Critical thinking
- Ability to form compelling arguments
- Time management
- Resilience

Qualities like these are likely to be useful in most roles, including those not directly linked to your subject knowledge and technical ability. Indeed, considering career options that rely mostly upon your broader skills might seem like a bold move, but opportunities certainly exist, especially in career areas with structured training schemes which hire based on transferable skills and train you on the job. Examples include the ancient historian who leveraged their problem-solving skills to get onto an accountancy graduate scheme, and a chemist who used the advocacy and influencing skills developed as a committee rep to secure an entry-level role in local government. As the second example shows, your broader skills don't just derive from undertaking your research; they also come from all the other things that you do 'around the edges' like teaching, committee roles, public engagement, part-time work, and so on.

As AI adoption and usage continues to rapidly grow and evolve across most sectors, these broader skills continue to come to the fore. For example, being an agile learner who can pick up new skills and methods quickly, plus being able to critically evaluate outputs and ask the right questions about data bias, are all the more crucial as AI in the workplace becomes both all-pervasive and more agentic.

Skills in navigating how research and universities work

An often-underappreciated skillset derived from experience in academia comes through your 'insider knowledge' around how academia and universities operate. This could include:

- Understanding what's involved in the academic research process, from proposal to funding to dissemination.
- The credibility and skills to communicate effectively with academics.
- Empathy with researchers' experience and needs.
- An understanding of teaching and pedagogy in higher education.

Since I began my career guidance work with researchers, I've seen increasing interest in what we might call 'academic-adjacent' career areas, be it roles in universities other than 'traditional' academic research and teaching, or roles in organisations that support research, such as independent research organisations (IROs) or funding bodies. An example of using this skillset for career transition is a former researcher who, after two postdocs in the medical humanities, drew on their experience of winning postdoctoral funding and their skills in communicating effectively with academics to move into a research support role helping academics to attract grant funding.

If items related to working in a university environment or supporting either students or research featured in the 'keep' column of your keep/lose/add profile, then exploring options using this skillset could help generate some ideas. Getting involved in other types of teaching in your institution (for example, in areas like skill development, academic writing, maths support, or career development) could be a way of experimenting with other types of student-facing work, whilst getting involved in things like public engagement or outreach could help you to explore types of work which happen at the intersection of higher education and the outside world. This could help you to explore career options that exist within higher education beyond academic research and teaching.

Connecting with people at your current university or institution working in roles other than research and teaching could also help you to explore possibilities. Perhaps there are staff in professional services, support roles, or other departments whose work overlaps with your interests and experience: seek opportunities to find out more about their work, be it through events, staff networks, collaborating with them, or even approaching them directly. A common mistake that researchers make when considering such options is treating 'academic-adjacent' roles as a homogenous category, failing to appreciate the breadth and variety of professions involved. Getting a realistic view of what is involved in, and required for, different roles is therefore crucial, not only to determine which ones fit your experience and priorities, but also to understand how your professional identity and relationship with academia may shift in these roles, despite still being based in a university environment.

Your other skills, experience, and interests

When generating career ideas, it's important to remember that you are more than just your research. Career possibilities could well exist at the intersections between the skills gained from your academic work and the experience, knowledge, and interests that you have developed beyond it. In fact, your unique combination of knowledge or skills that you've built through both your academic work and other pursuits could make you an ideal candidate for roles that could be a great fit. An example of this is the electronic engineer who blended technical expertise developed through their research on radar with a personal interest in media and journalism, landing a job as a research and development engineer for a broadcasting company. Rather than dismissing your previous work or outside interests as 'irrelevant,' consider what types of work or employers might value your unique package.

Get to work

It's now time to apply what we've learned about doctoral and postdoctoral skills to your own situation. Listing your own skills can be tricky, especially if you struggle with confidence or feel uncomfortable 'bigging yourself up.' So, we're going to take a different approach.

Exercise 3.1: Hiring another 'you'

Imagine you are going off on a nice, long sabbatical and need to hire someone else to carry on with your current research project in your place. Or, if you're not currently research active, imagine having to hire someone to do the project you most recently completed. Go through each of the six types of skillsets (or as many of them as are relevant), and list what that person would need. Ideally, start every item with 'you will need.' Table 3.1 gives you a template to use for your answers, using an example based on a real research project.

If you struggle to 'talk up' your own skills, listing them in the second person (using 'you will need' instead of 'I am good at') as Table 3.1 shows can help you escape self-deprecation and uncover the great package that you bring. Remember, by describing the skills needed from the person taking over from you, **you are also describing yourself**.

Table 3.1 Breaking down skills based on an example research project

Skillset	*Requirements*
Subject-specific knowledge	• You will need a good understanding of cardiac science. • You will need a good grasp of the different receptors on heart cells and how they work (cardiac pharmacology).
Research skills and methods	• You will need experience in lab techniques including western blotting, metabolism assays, cell culture, and cell contraction studies.
Usage of specialist equipment and technologies	• You will need a good level of experience in using electrophoresis equipment and cell contraction assays. • You will need to be able to programme a thermocycler.

(*Continued*)

Table 3.1 (Continued)

Skillset	*Requirements*
Data analysis skills	• You will need to be proficient in writing basic MATLAB code. • You will need be confident in choosing the most appropriate statistical tests.
Broader 'transferable' skills	• You will need strong skills in presenting data both orally and graphically. • You will need to have the ability to write clearly for a scientific audience. • You will also need the skills to present research in an accessible way to non-experts. • You will need good interpersonal skills for teaching and mentoring.
Skills in navigating how research and universities work	• You will need to be resourceful, with the initiative to identify new sources of research funding and other resources. • You will need to be able to collaborate with other research groups and understand how these groups work.
Other interests and experience	• You'll need a passion for engaging the public with science, e.g. through demonstrations and displays. • You'll need the patience and teaching skills to tutor students one-to-one.

As well as doing this for your research, you can also do it for any previous jobs you have had, as shown in the final row of Table 3.1. Potential career opportunities could lie at the intersections between your different skill types, or in the overlaps of the skills gained from your previous work and those developed through your research experience. To round off this chapter then, let's look at how you can start to spot these opportunities.

Case study

Finding connections between your different skills and interests can seem daunting if you're starting from scratch, so it can help to start by considering some examples.

Below are two simplified case studies from real doctoral graduates, outlining the skills and interests each person was most keen to draw on in their future work. Even though the people featured in the case studies may not be from your academic discipline, considering their examples – and those of other people you come across – is a valuable starting point. This exercise is about training you to think creatively about how different types of skills and interests can be combined into potential career ideas.

Exercise 3.2: Spotting career connections

For the case studies presented in Tables 3.2 and 3.3, consider the following questions:

- Which of their skills and interests did each person draw upon to move into what they are doing now?
- Can you think of any other options they could have pursued, using different combinations of their skills and interests?

Suggested 'answers' can be found at the end of this chapter.

Table 3.2 Case study from doctoral graduate Hanan

Subject-specific knowledge	*Research skills and methods*	*Broader 'transferable' skills and experience*	*Skills in navigating how research and universities work*	*Role secured*
PhD Education, Philosophy and, Religion Identity construction and experiences of Muslim students in UK Higher Education. General subject knowledge in theology, philosophy, and education	Interviews and focus groups: skilled in rapport and trust building Thematic analysis	Teaching skills: especially from a module about 'learning journeys' Experience mentoring students – offering guidance Library services adviser experience Freelance research experience on progression of aspiring leaders from under-represented ethnic backgrounds	Understanding and empathy of what it's like to go through a PhD/ do academic research Understanding of the research process	**Researcher Training and Development Officer** Planning and delivery of training programmes to support researchers' career development and help them to thrive Ensuring that the training meets researchers' needs Setting up networks and mentoring opportunities for international researchers

Table 3.3 Case study from doctoral graduate Brendan

Subject-specific knowledge	*Research methods/ analytical skills*	*Broader 'transferable' skills*	*'Extra' skills and interests*	*Role secured*
PhD Biomedical Science: the role of sex hormones on the heart General subject knowledge in physiology and cardiovascular science.	Protein analysis, e.g. Western blotting Statistics Cell culture Designing & running experiments on cardiac dynamics	Teaching & public engagement skills: Coordinated science communication events Producing educational materials: experience gained through university teaching and tutoring	Interest in aviation and flight: member of a gliding club	**Editorial role with a medical education company:** Liaising with scientific authors Validating accuracy of articles Developing resources to upskill medical professionals

Exercise 3.3: Map your skills

Now you've seen a few examples, try it for yourself!

- Create a table like those in Exercise 3.2 to complete for your own skills and experience. You can use the items from your 'hiring another you' exercise to help with this.
- Try combining some of your own preferred skills and interests together to come up with some initial career ideas. Use some simple combinations to get started, such as:
    - What roles might combine your [subject expertise in X] and also involve [broader skill Y]?"
    - If you combined [subject knowledge in X] with [your 'extra' interest in Y]: what could that look like?
    - What kinds of organisations might need [research skill X] and are also linked to your [interest in Y]?
    - If you're really stuck, who might be able to help you with these kinds of questions?
- If you're struggling, use the LinkedIn tips in the 'what does this mean for you' section of this chapter to get some inspiration based on what others with your skills have done, or refer to the tips that former doctoral and postdoctoral researchers share in Chapter 4 regarding how they focused their job hunt. You could also ask an AI large language model like Copilot or Chat GPT for ideas, though make sure you sense-check any results by cross-checking them with real job descriptions or, even better, talking to people who do the roles suggested (see the message templates in Chapter 4 to help you reach out).

Takeaways

- Several studies show that doctoral graduates attribute their job success beyond academia to the skills gained during their doctoral research.
- Six key types of skills developed in academia that are valued by employers are:
  - Subject-specific knowledge: Your expertise may be highly valued not only in academia, but also in a range of other industries where specialist knowledge is essential.
  - Research skills and methods: These are transferable to a variety of roles and settings beyond academia.
  - Expertise in using specialist equipment and technologies such as lab consumables, scientific instruments, and specialist software: This can also be leveraged for career transition beyond academia, including for roles with companies who make and sell these products.
  - Data analysis: Such skills, including coding languages and other analytical methods, represent another skillset applicable beyond academia.
  - Navigating academic systems: Insider knowledge about academic research processes and how universities and research institutes work are also valuable, especially for professional services roles in higher education and roles which link up academia with industry and other external bodies and organisations.
  - Broader transferable skills: Skills such as problem-solving, attention to detail, critical thinking, and an ability to form compelling arguments can be applied in many settings.

- Thinking creatively about how some of your skills and interests could combine into potential next steps is a valuable career exploration skill.

Exercise 3.2 'answers'

Hanan's case study – Table 3.2

The role that Hanan moved into mostly combines her experience and interests in mentoring, guidance, and teaching, with the rapport-building skills from her research methods and her understanding of what undertaking academic research entails. Hanan's new role involves identifying researchers' needs and delivering tailored support that enables their professional development.

Potential other 'combinations' for Hanan could include:

- Research methods + educational expertise = social research or policy role for a government department or research consultancy.
- Teaching and mentoring skills + experience of freelance research looking at progression of future leaders = training and development role in a training company or in-house in a private -sector company.
- General subject knowledge in education and/or theology & religion + teaching skills = education or engagement role with an educational or faith-related charity.

Brendan's case study – Table 3.3

Brendan mostly drew on his experience of communicating science to a range of audiences (from public engagement) and his skills in producing educational materials gained through teaching and tutoring to move into an editorial role with a medical education company. Although the job doesn't involve 'doing science,' Brendan's scientific knowledge and his ability to keep up to date on the literature are crucial to this role.

Other possible 'combinations' that Brendan considered include:

- Specialist knowledge in cardiology + experience running experiments on cardiac function = technical specialist role with a cardiac-focused MedTech company.
- Specialist knowledge in physiology + passion for aviation = scientist role for an aerospace company focused on human physiology during flight.
- Science communication skills + experience producing educational resources = research communication role for a disease-related charity.

References

Boyd, R. and McAlinden, S. (2016) *PhD Study to Employment: Experiences of Transition*. Available at: https://luminate.prospects.ac.uk/phd-study-to-employment-experiences-of-transition [Accessed 9 December 2024].

Bryan, B. and Guccione, K. (2018) 'Was it worth it? A qualitative exploration into graduate perceptions of doctoral value,' *Higher Education Research & Development*, 37(6), pp. 1124–1140. doi: 10.1080/07294360.2018.1479378.

Council for Industry and Higher Education (2010) *Talent Fishing: What Businesses Want from Postgraduates*. London: CIHE. Available at: https://www.ncub.co.uk/reports/talent-fishing-what-businesses-want-from-postgraduates.html [Accessed 9 December 2024].

Diamond, A., Ball, C., Vorley, T., Hughes, T., Moreton, R., Howe, P. and Nathwani, T. (2014) *The Impact of Doctoral Careers* [online]. Leicester: CFE Research. Available at: https://www.ncub.co.uk/insight/the-impact-of-doctoral-careers/ [Accessed 20 October 2024].

Elias, P., Purcell, K., Durbin, S., Davies, R. and Warren, S. (2005) *The Employment of Social Science PhDs in Academic and Non-Academic Jobs: Research Skills and Postgraduate Training*. Swindon: Economic and Social Research Council. Available at: https://warwick.ac.uk/fac/soc/ier/publications/2005/final_draft_socsci_phds_06_june_2005.pdf [Accessed 20 October 2024].

Guerin, C. (2020) 'Stories of moving on: HASS PhD graduates' motivations and career trajectories inside and beyond academia,' *Arts and Humanities in Higher Education*, 19(3), pp. 304–324. doi: 10.1177/1474022219834448.

Hancock, S. (2021) 'What is known about doctoral employment? Reflections from a UK study and directions for future research,' *Journal of Higher Education Policy and Management*, 43(5), pp. 520–536. doi: 10.1080/1360080X.2020.1870027.

Lee, H.F., Miozzo, M. and Laredo, P. (2010) 'Career patterns and competences of PhDs in science and engineering in the knowledge economy: the case of graduates from a UK research-based university,' *Research Policy*, 39(7), pp. 869–881. doi: 10.1016/j.respol.2010.05.001.

McAlpine, L. and Inouye, K. (2022) 'What value do PhD graduates offer? An organizational case study,' *Higher Education Research & Development*, 41(5), pp. 1648–1663. doi: 10.1080/07294360.2021.1945546.

Muurlink, O., Chen, L., Boorman, R., Pearson, D. and Cohen, G. (2024) 'Stakeholder perceptions of what industry wants from doctoral students: a systematic literature review,' *Higher Education Research & Development*, 43(4), pp. 952–965. doi: 10.1080/07294360.2023.2269871.

Paolo, A.D. and Mañé, F. (2016) 'Misusing our talent? Overeducation, overskilling and skill underutilisation among Spanish PhD graduates,' *The Economic and Labour Relations Review*, 27(4), pp. 432–452. doi: 10.1177/1035304616657479.

Peacey, S. and Romijn, L. (2026) *What Do Postdocs Do Next?* [online]. Cambridge: University of Cambridge Careers Service. Available at: https://www.careers.cam.ac.uk/careers-support-postdocs/what-do-postdocs-do-next [Accessed 21 January 2026].

Pham, T. (2025) 'What really contributes to employability of PhD graduates in uncertain labour markets?' *Globalisation, Societies and Education*, 23(2), pp. 435–446. doi: 10.1080/14767724.2023.2192908

Rubio, M. and Hooley, T. (2010) *Recruiting Researchers: Survey of Employer Practice 2009* [online]. Cambridge: The Careers Research and Advisory Centre. Available at: https://hdl.handle.net/10545/583862 [Accessed 1 October 2024].

4 Tackling common questions about careers beyond academia

Starting to explore your future beyond academia can bring up as many questions as it does answers. For example, if you're coming towards the end of a doctorate or are employed on an academic contract, job-hunting timelines can feel much less clear than they do for 'regular' graduates. Types and levels of roles can also feel difficult to navigate; whilst 'graduate' roles are an obvious next step after a bachelor's degree, knowing which roles to aim at after working at doctoral or postdoctoral level can feel much more ambiguous.

Before we look specifically at finding and forging opportunities beyond academia, we're going to take an interlude to address some of the most persistent questions that plague researchers when it comes to weighing up possible next steps. To give these key questions the attention they deserve, we're going to break from the structure of the rest of the book so far and tackle them in turn, featuring examples of how real-life researchers have navigated each issue.

DOI: 10.4324/9781003589785-5

Making career decisions

How do I decide what to apply for?

There is no single secret 'trick' for deciding how to focus your job hunt. I've seen researchers use a range of strategies to narrow down their searches, many of which have led them into rewarding new careers. Case studies 4.1–4.4 show stories of how real former doctoral and postdoctoral researchers decided what to apply for; read through them, and pick out the main points you think might help you to focus your search.

You will notice that each took a slightly different approach. In case study 4.1, Victoria outlines how she chose some options she felt might keep her linked to academia, then used the interview process itself to narrow down what would suit her best, interviewing potential employers as much as they were interviewing her. Case study 4.2 shows how Sophie initially worked out what aspects of her postdoc research role she most enjoyed, then used career advice resources like blogs and case studies to identify options that might align with this. Rather than narrowing down his search to specific roles, Cameron explains in case study 4.3 how he focused on applying for positions that would most consistently use the skills he'd enjoyed using in his PhD. Finally, in case study 4.4, Ben demonstrates how he evaluated his wants and needs for his next steps, and narrowed down his options in line with these.

Nevertheless, **talking to people** was crucial for all four of them. Whether it was conversations within the recruitment process, chatting with friends, meeting careers advisers, setting up calls with potential employers, having discussions with people working in roles they were interested in, or all of the above, gathering information through real-life conversations is a theme that unites all the stories.

Case study 4.1 Deciding on options

Victoria
PhD in Classics
Now working in Professional Services
in Higher Education

I knew I wanted to stay linked to academia, but not necessarily as an academic, due to the sheer competitiveness and dearth of jobs in my subject area, and because I was never that drawn to teaching. This led me to looking at academic-adjacent jobs (professional services in higher education) and academic publishing.

Initially I applied for both and thought I would use the interview process to get a feel for what might be best for me. Early on, I had an interview with an academic publishing company; it was a useful experience because both my interviewers and I realised that it wasn't really for me. This was actually quite a positive experience! They knew not to waste time progressing my application because we'd discovered that this wasn't right for me. I remember feeling quite positive afterwards, especially as the interviewers were nice about it. This is part of what the interview process is for, after all.

From then on, I decided to focus on applying for higher education roles, especially those focused on research impact. A lot of opportunities in this area were being created in the UK at the time, and I was drawn to this option as it fit my experience and would allow me to work closely with academic staff and their research, which is what I wanted. When I started getting interviews for these types of roles, even when I wasn't successful, my experiences in the interviews confirmed this was the route I wanted to take. I arranged chats with several people in the same or similar roles at the university where I did my PhD, which was helpful and also affirmed my decision.

For me then, it was taking action – that is, talking to people and going for interviews – that helped me decide on my focus, rather than just assuming what I might enjoy.

Case study 4.2 Deciding on options

Sophie
PhD and three-years postdoc in Biomedical Sciences
Now working in Medical Communications

I started preparing to move my career beyond academia by connecting with careers advisors within my academic institution. I was signposted to several great resources about the type of roles which exist outside of academia, including blog posts and articles about what other PhDs and postdocs had gone on to do. Alongside considering these, I sat down and made a list of the things I enjoyed about my research role, as well as the things I disliked about it, to help inform my priorities. Additionally, I created a 'skillset bank' where I recorded specific examples of my skills, including those I wanted to carry in using in my next job.

Finally, I began to network on LinkedIn. I reached out to people in a variety of roles that I thought might be interesting and managed to schedule information-gathering interviews with a range of individuals. I found these sessions especially useful to help narrow down my search to a few types of roles, one of which was Medical Writer.

I initially saw my current position – Medical Writer in a pharmaceutical company – on LinkedIn; I reached out to people working within the company and was able to schedule an informal chat with a member of the wider team. This gave me great insights into what the company was after, as well as ensuring that it was the position for me!

In addition to helping me decide my focus, this process also really helped me once I got to interview. For example, during my interview I was able to ask my interviewer about a particular news story related to a recent FDA approval; this highlighted that I was serious about moving into the industry, that I was committed to learning about the company, and helped me come across as well prepared. I think everything I did throughout the process of deciding to focus on medical writing ultimately contributed to me being offered the role out of over 600 applicants!

Case study 4.3 Deciding on options

Cameron
PhD Sport and Exercise Sciences
Now working for a local authority

Before I started my PhD, I thought that I would likely either stay in academia, or that I would move into industry and work in professional sport, but ultimately I was open-minded about what I might do next.

To decide on what types of roles to apply for, I tried to speak to people with careers in the fields I was interested in to gain a deeper understanding of the day-to-day reality of the job and pathways for progression. When it came to looking at and applying for jobs, I decided to put more time into fewer applications, really tailoring my CV and cover letter or personal statement to the role, rather than casting the net wide and sending out lots of generic applications. Since I didn't have very specific roles in mind and had broad career interests, I allowed myself to be guided by roles that caught my eye and sounded interesting. I also focused on roles that required skills that I used during my PhD, and that I had particularly enjoyed and felt confident using, rather than narrowing down to specific job titles.

My role now is a Research Fellow, but it is with local authority rather than an academic institution. It lets me use the skills I was interested in using, such as reading academic literature and synthesising the evidence in a variety of ways. The role also involves training and upskilling local authority staff to develop their critical appraisal skills and build their confidence in working with academic literature, the goal being to improve the use of evidence-based decision making within the local council. Teaching and supervising undergraduate and Master's students definitely gave me the experience and confidence needed for this training element of my role.

Case study 4.4 Deciding on options

Ben
PhD History
Now working in central government service

At the beginning of my final year as a doctoral researcher, I started thinking about *what I wanted and what I needed from a role*. I wanted to work on something that I could be proud of, that I would have a lasting interest in, and that would offer clear and structured career progression. I also wanted to capitalise on the skills I had developed in my nine years as a historian.

On top of this, I worked out that I had three needs: a salary that allowed me to live independently; a start-date close to when I completed my doctorate; and a role that would offer support in adapting to a new profession.

Through my academic work in Roman history, I had been researching and had been interested in politics and public opinion for almost a decade by this point, so I was particularly drawn to politically-adjacent public service roles. It was through talking to a close friend who was going through the same process towards the end of their doctorate, and through meeting with a careers adviser at my university, that I also started to consider graduate training schemes. Two particular graduate schemes in the UK met all my criteria: one was in local government and the other was in central government service. So, I applied to those schemes and secured a place on the latter.

In short, I decided which roles to focus on by understanding and prioritising my wants and needs, understanding my limits, and using my network to help me identify possible roles based on my criteria.

What if I make the wrong choice?

I speak to many doctoral and postdoctoral researchers who put a lot of pressure on themselves to get their career choice after academia 'right first time.' Choosing what to do next may feel like a huge decision, especially if you have a partner, dependants, and other responsibilities to consider. However, as Burnett and Evans describe in their popular book *Designing Your Life*, your career isn't necessarily a 'problem' to which there is only one single solution (2018: 77), and it's unlikely that choosing one role or one industry will be categorically 'right,' whilst choosing others will be 'wrong.' There may be many 'right' ways for your professional life to take shape, that will let you use the parts of yourself that you most value whilst fitting well with the rest of your life.

Remember, you aren't 'locked in' to the first job you move into beyond academia. In many sectors, opportunities to move sideways and upwards are often more available than they are within academia, where high competition for few roles might feel like you're waiting for someone to retire until a new opening becomes available. Rather than pressuring yourself to make the 'right decision' first time, instead, work out what 'wrong choice' would mean for you. Would it be moving into a job that conflicts with your deep-seated values? Would it mean not being able to use the skills you want to apply to your work every day? Would it mean having little time for friends, family, and other pursuits? When you can articulate what 'wrong choice' means for you, focus on finding out whether the options you are considering are likely to align or clash with this.

That said, even if you've done your research, this doesn't grant you a crystal ball to predict your professional future. Things beyond your control like unanticipated changes in management or company restructures may impact your workload and focus, taking your role away from your preferences and expectations. Chapter 7 will explain how you can then use your keep/lose/add profile as a compass, to reassert agency over your career and bring it back into alignment with what's important to you. In case study 4.5 doctoral graduate Victoria, who we heard from previously in case study 4.1, offers tips for researchers who fear making the 'wrong choice' about their first position beyond academia.

Case study 4.5 Fearing you'll make the 'wrong choice'

Victoria
PhD Classics
Now working in Professional Services in Higher Education

Rather than trying to overthink things, at some point you need to just go for it. You won't know properly if something is right for you until you experience it. Besides, even if you end up feeling like you've made the 'wrong choice,' you don't have to stay. When you first start a job, it's likely you'll be on a probationary period and as I always like to say, that's a time for you to put *them* on probation as much as they put you on probation...! That time is for you to get a feel for your new colleagues and for the role. If you don't like it, you can leave. It won't have an indelible impact on your professional life (unless you do it so often that it becomes a pattern, maybe). If your next potential employer asks why you moved on, you can tell them that the role wasn't what you expected, that you learned that role wasn't for you but that it showed you that what you actually want to do now is what they are offering, which is why you're now talking to them.

Making connections

How do I reach out on LinkedIn without seeming creepy?

Actively exploring opportunities and growing your network beyond academia may mean reaching out to people you don't know yet, or that you don't know very well. This might involve:

- Sending messages on LinkedIn to PhD alumni from your university or former members of your institution to see if they'd be happy to share how they got into their current role.
- Emailing someone you met at a conference to follow up about your interest in their company.
- Messaging someone who is advertising a job to set up an informal chat about the role and other potential openings.

It's normal to feel nervous or uncomfortable about making such approaches, especially if you're worried about 'bothering' people. To prepare, therefore, put yourself in the position of the recipient. Imagine, for example, that a Master's student who is considering doing a doctorate, or a doctoral researcher considering a postdoc, reached out to you in a similar way. They want to see if you'd be willing to offer any tips on the application process. Think:

- What would make you more likely to respond? This could include:
  - Clearly saying why they are contacting you.
  - Having something in common, e.g. you studied or worked at the same university or institute, or that you met briefly at an event.
  - Asking specific questions that you don't have to go away and look up and can answer from your own experience.
- What would make you more likely to ignore the message?
  - Not explaining why they chose to reach out to you specifically.

- A vague request that requires more questions to clarify, e.g. 'I am interested in a career in X, please guide me.'
- Asking multiple, complex questions that you couldn't just respond to whilst you were, for example, riding the bus home.

Use your answers to compose a template message that you can use when reaching out to people. Case study 4.6 gives some examples which stay within the 200-character limit allowed for a personalised connection request when using the free version of LinkedIn.

Case study 4.6 Example LinkedIn connection messages

Template

Dear [name]. I'm a PhD in [X subject] at [X university/ institute]; I noticed you [make a personal connection with them that shows you aren't a bot]. I'd love to find out more about [your path into X career/ your company's priorities]. Would it be possible to connect? Thanks, [name].

Example reaching out to alumni

Dear Gustaph, I'm a PhD at Example University and saw you also once worked in Dr Li's group. I'd love to find out more about your path into UX research. Would it be possible to connect? Thanks, Blanka

Example reaching out to someone in a company of interest

Dear Marco, I saw your post about ChemCo Ltd expanding its renewable energy team. With a strong interest in renewables & five years' experience in biomass processing, I'd love to find out more. Thanks, Mae

Job hunting timelines

When should I start actively applying for jobs beyond academia?

Your timeline is likely to depend on several factors, including how much 'groundwork' you've put into addressing the emotions of career change (Chapter 1), understanding your motivations and options (Chapters 2 and 3), developing your network (Chapter 5) and translating your experience effectively for employers (Chapter 6).

Elvidge et al. suggest that for postdocs leaving academia, the average time taken to switch roles is around six months (2017: 165). If you have already done your groundwork, this may be a realistic timeframe; however, if you are still getting to grips with the emotional and practical aspects of transitioning beyond academia, the process may take longer. Here are the main factors to consider when working out your timeline:

1 Your circumstances: For example, whether your finances would allow you a 'gap' between the end of your doctorate/current contract and starting a job,

whether balancing your thesis write-up alongside a new job would be feasible for you, and so on.

2 Your current programme/position. You may feel pressure to delay applying for jobs beyond academia because you're worried about letting down supervisors or principal investigators, especially if you were named on your project grant. While these concerns are understandable, they are not always insurmountable, and although some employers may want a vacancy filled immediately, others may be more flexible. I've worked with several researchers whose new employers have delayed their start date or let them start part-time until after they have wrapped up their current research (e.g. see Ellen's story in case study 4.8). If sufficient time is left on a grant, your PI or manager may be able to recruit short-term cover if you do leave before the end, so not leaving things too late could help you both out in the long run. Knowing the notice period required on your current contract and being open about accepting another job offer as soon as possible can help you balance feelings of professional responsibility with doing what's right for you.

3 Recruitment processes and employer's expectations. For example, opportunities like graduate schemes, structured training programmes, or other openings where employers recruit lots of new staff in one go may have long recruitment processes. In some cases, you may only start the job up to a year after you completed the initial application stage, so make sure you research typical recruitment processes for the kinds of roles you are interested in well in advance. In case study 4.7, Ollie summarises the timeline he worked to when applying for such roles to start after his

doctorate. In contrast, in case study 4.8, Ellen outlines how her timeline worked when applying for jobs with a more standard, shorter recruitment process. It is also worth noting that in some sectors (particularly in STEM, where a PhD is required for a certain role), employers may be hesitant to interview candidates who have not yet submitted their thesis. Knowing in advance if this is the case for employers you are targeting is therefore crucial as it may influence your timelines.

4 Market realities: Talk to recent doctoral graduates or former postdocs who have recently started jobs beyond academia to get a sense of how long it took them. Focus on people in relevant roles and locations, as timelines can vary. Use these conversations to build a realistic picture of current hiring conditions, whilst acknowledging that individual experiences will differ. Be wary of fixating solely on negative accounts; instead, look for patterns across multiple sources.

5 Your availability. Once you have the information you need regarding your circumstances, your current notice period/rough submission or viva dates (or equivalent), and any specifics around the recruitment timelines and expectations of your target employers, establish when will be feasible for you to start a job. Being able to tell an employer 'I will be available to start full-time work from the end of January,' or 'I will be available for part-time work from January to April, after which I will be available full-time' will help them to see if you fit into their hiring timeline or not. If you are unsure whether your timeline aligns with an employer's, contact the person advertising the vacancy or make your availability clear in your application. Stating your availability could at least open

negotiations. If you can afford a gap before your next role, and the opportunities you are applying for do not follow fixed recruitment cycles (such as graduate schemes), then beginning applications around three months before your availability begins may be feasible. However, in unpredictable job markets where factors such as layoffs and generative AI usage increase the number of applications per vacancy, even well-qualified candidates can take longer than expected to secure a role. If you cannot afford a gap, or you are targeting a sector or location where competition is high, it is wise to start earlier: six months in advance or more, depending on your notice period. Consider the possibility that your job search may take longer than hoped and build a buffer, such as savings to cover living costs, or contingency plans like short-term work to maintain some income, structure, and sense of purpose.

Case study 4.7 Applying for roles with long recruitment processes

Ollie
PhD in Nutrition and Exercise Metabolism
Now working in consulting

After becoming interested in consulting a few years into my doctorate, I realised I needed to be organised. Depending on the company and type of consulting, it can be a particularly demanding application process, so I started preparing for this early by attending recruitment and information events held by consulting firms, both at my university and independently. From what I learned at these events, I planned the following timeline:

- Approximately one year before applying: I drew up a shortlist of companies and their application timelines. I knew that in my country, most large consulting firms would open applications in September for intake the following year, whilst smaller companies would usually open applications a few months before potential start dates.
- The August before I wanted to start a job: I set aside time each week to practise for mathematical and numerical tests and case study interviews. This was really demanding whilst also finishing up my PhD experiments and completing my thesis. To help, I started my PhD work early in the day and finished each day by working on interview preparation, aiming for at least two hours per day (which I increased when I got invited to interviews).
- September to February: applying for jobs and going for interviews. This was a very busy period as I was also writing up my thesis which I submitted in December!
- February: I received two job offers. Although they started at different times of the year, both would allow me to do my viva and make any necessary corrections before starting the job.

My main advice would be to understand the timelines for the roles you are interested in as early as possible, especially if you're considering options like consulting in which some applications open way in advance of start dates. I spoke to many people interested in consulting who found themselves only preparing for interviews a few days in advance, and others who could only apply for a few jobs because many deadlines had closed. When looking at a career with such a rigorous and time-consuming application process, set aside regular time to prepare, as this can't just be crammed into a few days before an interview. Small amounts of work on a regular basis with like-minded people is the best way to approach this.

Case study 4.8 Applying for roles with shorter recruitment processes

Ellen
PhD English Literature
Now working in the arts and cultural sector

I knew from the start of my doctorate that I wanted a career in the arts sector. I started thinking about jobs with around 18 months left of my PhD which at times, I admit, was a distraction. However, it allowed me to survey the scene and see patterns in the types of jobs in my preferred sector so when the time came, I was ready to go.

I started job hunting about six months before my thesis submission date (end of September). This was a little early as most jobs had a start date a couple months before I submitted, and I didn't want to start so soon. So, I instead spent April-June working on my CV, a general personal statement outline, and updating my LinkedIn, as well as keeping an eye on job sites, which was really beneficial. I had lots of people look over my CV (including a careers adviser and some friends) and developed multiple versions that I could tailor for different audiences. Towards the end of June, I found two jobs that I loved the look of; I applied, and in August I got interviews for both, then an offer for one of them which I accepted.

The employer wanted me to start my new job in early September, but I had planned to take a month out between submitting my PhD and starting a job. With a careers adviser's help, I drafted an email to explain my situation and negotiate my start-date and terms. I managed to get my new employer to agree to move the start-date to mid-September, and for me to work part-time for the first six weeks. This allowed me to start in the role gradually and remotely whilst I finished my thesis and recuperated after submitting!

Ultimately, your job-hunting timeline is down to your needs. If looking for a job will distract you detrimentally from the research you are finishing up, perhaps wait until the latter stages to start job searching (depending on your circumstances). However, keeping an eye on job boards and signing up to job alerts doesn't hurt. After all, if your so-called dream job is advertised a few months earlier than you'd like, the employer (like mine) might be flexible around start dates and terms, so there's no harm in going for it if you have the capacity.

How can I manage time pressures in my job hunt?

If the end of your doctorate, current contract, or visa duration is imminent, you may feel under pressure to find a new job as soon as possible. If you are in this situation, be sure to:

- Identify and make use of any career guidance, researcher development, or staff development provision within your institution that can help you to explore options.
- Take time to understand your contract, including its terms, conditions, and expiry date. Although you may feel very committed to your current role or project, remember that depending on terms and conditions, it is likely that you have the right to resign and move jobs before your contract ends (Elvidge et al., 2017: 163).
- Be aware of your rights. For example, if you are a member of staff approaching the end of your contract, ask your institution's HR department what redundancy pay you should expect, and how to receive this. Also, enquire about access to processes such as redeployment. If you are on a fixed-term contract (e.g. as a postdoc, contract researcher, or member of teaching staff), find out if your institution's HR team or similar offers consultations to discuss prospects for alternative options as you approach your contract end. Similarly, find out if your institution has a redeployment policy and familiarise yourself with it. This could give you priority for internal roles not just within

your department but in other parts of the university too, including professional services and 'academic adjacent' roles.

- Consider which job-hunting activities are likely to give you the greatest return on your time investment. Your instinct may be that you don't have time for networking and that you're better off spending time sending out applications in response to as many job adverts as possible. However, as we will see in Chapter 5, being hired through networking may have potential advantages including a shorter and smoother recruitment process. Take stock of your existing networks, therefore, and think how they can help you expedite your job search.
- Make use of potential 'dead time' for your job hunt. For example, send LinkedIn connections or email current contacts whilst you're on public transport, or listen to researcher careers podcasts whilst walking to get inspiration about potential options, such as:
    - 'Careers in Your Ears': a careers podcast for PhD students and research staff created by King's College London
    - 'Beyond The Thesis with Papa PhD': featuring interviews with doctoral researchers, postdocs, and academics now working in diverse areas of the job market.
- Make sure you understand other restrictions and legislation that may affect when and how you can start a new job, including visa restrictions. In case study 4.9, doctoral graduate Qiu outlines how she navigated this.

Case study 4.9 Navigating the job hunt as an international researcher

Qiu
PhD Applied Linguistics
Now working in Professional Services in Higher Education

First of all, make sure you are fully aware of the visa options open to you in the relevant country and the timelines required for applying for these. For example, I was initially on a student visa in the UK so to stay there and work, I knew I needed to switch to another kind of visa that would allow me to do this. Before my student visa expired, I focused on applying for jobs that could sponsor a relevant working visa, but didn't manage to secure one in time. I then initiated plan B which was to apply for the UK's graduate visa because I knew this was also an option, so make sure you know what your visa options are and whether you have potential contingency plans.

Linked to this is making sure you consider all your options. For example, although I primarily focused on applying for roles likely to offer sponsorship, I also applied for part-time roles (that I could cover with my graduate visa) as a way of getting a foot in the door. This paid off as I was initially offered a professional services job in a university on a six-month contract, before then securing a permanent position at another university. Still though, this wasn't straightforward: when I was offered the permanent role I tried to negotiate visa sponsorship straight away, but the salary was slightly below the threshold required for this in the UK. The employer took a few days to confirm whether they could raise it; unfortunately, this wasn't possible so I would have to continue using my graduate visa for now. However, they did indicate that after a year in the role, my salary should increase by just enough to qualify me for visa sponsorship, so I accepted the job with this hope. It has been quite a stressful process, but hopefully it will work out in time. So, whilst my example is UK-specific, make sure you understand the equivalent options in your target country, keep an open mind about options, and actively negotiate potential outcomes with employers.

Overall, if you are an international researcher who needs visa sponsorship to work, be upfront about your visa needs. Some job descriptions specify whether they offer sponsorship, but many don't. In these cases, reach out for clarification to help prioritise your applications. If you receive an offer, always ask about visa sponsorship before accepting. Failing to clarify visa sponsorship and salary requirements before accepting an offer can leave you in a weaker position for negotiations if issues arise later. Prioritise applying for visa sponsored roles but also have backup plans that align with your long-term career goals. Don't sacrifice personal development just to secure a visa. Plus, visa policies change over time, so make sure you're clear on what you want.

Decoding job adverts

Am I wasting my doctorate if I apply for graduate-level roles?

This question is most relevant if you are job hunting in countries where some employers have a structured annual intake of graduates through 'graduate schemes': structured training programmes that are often open to graduates of all levels, and in some cases from a wide range of different subject areas.

The answer depends on what you're looking for from your next career step. If you've completed a doctorate and/or a postdoc, you may feel that your days of going to work with 21-year-olds are over. A lot of researchers I work with express fear that their higher-level qualifications and experience will be 'wasted' if they apply for roles that, in theory, they could have been eligible for straight out of their first degree.

That said, there are some circumstances in which I've seen researchers embrace 'graduate-level' roles, or structured graduate training schemes, as part of their career transition. These circumstances include:

- Having little, or no, work experience beyond academia. In this case, graduate-level openings can be a good way of training on the job, helping to ease the learning curve that can come with moving from an academic to a more commercial working environment.
- Moving into a line of work that is not directly related to your research or previous experience. Programmes like graduate schemes often offer structured routes

into certain sectors for people from a wide variety of academic backgrounds.
- Testing out different roles within an organisation to work out where your interests lie. Some structured graduate schemes offer the chance to 'rotate' around different teams and functions to gain different experiences and work out where you might see yourself longer term.
- Choosing graduate schemes with companies in which PhD graduates tend to progress more quickly, due to the value placed on increased maturity and high-level skills.

If you count yourself in any one of these camps, then a graduate-level opportunity could be one way to kick-start your career beyond academia. In case study 4.10 we hear again from doctoral graduate Ben about how this worked for him.

Case study 4.10 Moving from doctorate to graduate scheme

Ben
PhD History
Now working in central government service

After my PhD, I was interested in moving into work related to politics and the public sector. Although my research was related to political themes and public opinion, I had limited formal work experience in this field, so I knew that it would help to find roles that took into consideration the fact that I was changing profession and would offer continued support and training through that transition. For me, that all-but ruled out direct applications for early-career positions, as many appeared to require several years of professional experience, which, whether rightly or wrongly, I felt like I didn't have at the time.

Talking to a friend and a careers adviser prompted me to take serious notice of graduate schemes. Although many are notoriously competitive, several met all of my needs, and offered recognition that whilst I could bring some well-developed and relevant skills to the role, I would likely need support in adapting to a new profession.

Graduate schemes often have a tried-and-tested structure that systematically develops graduates through exposure to varied and increasingly challenging areas and projects. On the public sector graduate scheme that I joined, for example, I rotated to a different role and organisation every six or twelve months. Through those rotations, I worked with more organisations and with colleagues in a broader range of roles than I might otherwise have done had I not been on a structured scheme.

While working for one organisation, I provided the secretariat function for a governance body. This meant that I came into regular contact with representatives from other organisations, one of whom had a role that I thought sounded particularly interesting. I arranged a conversation with them, learned more about their organisation and their role, and decided that I wanted to take my career in a similar direction. Fortunately, a couple of 'rotations' later,

I was posted to that colleague's organisation and my suspicion that I would enjoy the work there was confirmed. So, towards the end of my time on the graduate scheme, I kept my eye out for a more permanent opportunity in that organisation and when one came up, I went for it.

For me, joining a graduate scheme worked exactly as it was meant to, providing a catalyst for learning, development, and networking.

What level of job can I apply for beyond academia?

Chris Caterine notes that one of the biggest challenges researchers face when moving into other sectors 'is the perception that you're overqualified for entry-level positions, but underqualified for more senior listings' (2020: 88). This can lead to uncertainties around what level of role is appropriate for you, and how to avoid pitching yourself too high or too low.

As with many common questions about transitioning from academia into other sectors, there is no black-and-white answer to this as it depends heavily on your experience and the sectors you are targeting. In my career guidance practice with researchers, however, I've devised a framework you can use to try to determine this for yourself.

Think of every job as having four major elements:

- Subject area: the academic subject(s) associated with the job and its context (if there are any).

- Work activities: the things you do in the job day-to-day.
- Environment: the setting you're working in and how this operates.
- Mission: the main goal(s) to which your work contributes (e.g. creating a product, delivering a service, etc.).

The more similar these four elements are to what you have done before, the more confidence an employer is likely to have that you can do what they need you to do. A high level of similarity therefore means that a 'Senior' or 'Manager' role may be realistic. One example of this is a doctoral researcher (without postdoc experience) who applied for a Senior Scientist role in a pharmaceutical company that was heavily focused on the biochemistry techniques they had used in their research. The subject area and the work activities were very similar to their past experience, whilst the environment was somewhat similar (although in industry, they were still lab-based). The mission of their work was different, contributing to developing drugs rather than doing basic science, but because the other elements were so similar they were offered the job, despite postdoctoral experience being listed as one of the selection criteria.

The more different a job's four elements are to what you've done before, the more likely it is that you'll have to start lower, perhaps at 'Scientist,' 'Officer,' 'Analyst,' or whatever the equivalent is in organisations to which you are applying. If most of the elements are significantly different, but it's a sector or organisation you're very keen to enter, then you may have to take it down again to 'Assistant' level (or equivalent). The more elements you try to change in your transition, the more likely it is that you may also have to initially compromise on salary. Trying to figure out the 'level' of roles beyond academia based on salary alone is tricky, as pay can vary significantly between sectors and regions. Depending on the relevance of your previous experience and your target sectors or roles, evidence does suggest that doctoral and postdoctoral training can carry 'opportunity costs,' where entering the labour market later may initially mean earning less than other colleagues of the same age (e.g. Kahn and Ginther, 2017; Wouterse et al., 2017).

Sometimes, you may receive mixed messages about which level of role is most appropriate. For example, I've seen some researchers who, to their surprise, have been shortlisted for more senior roles then they expected, but then miss out on interviews for more junior roles. This can depend on a range of factors such as who else applies, or which of the criteria are of highest priority for the employer. If you are unsure about how your experience aligns with the seniority of a role, reach out to the person advertising the role to find out which criteria are their priorities, or look up people who currently work in that type of role on LinkedIn to gauge what level of experience they had before moving into it. In case study 4.11, experienced recruiter Kate shares her tips on navigating uncertainties around what level of role may be most appropriate for you.

Case study 4.11 A recruiter's perspective

Kate
Early-Career Recruiter

It's no surprise that doctoral graduates are often confused as to where they 'fit' in sectors beyond academia, as it's likely that companies will take a range of different approaches to their recruitment. There is no 'one size fits all' answer as to what level of role you can, or should, go for.

Some organisations will be very specific about the level of experience needed for something like a graduate scheme versus an experienced hire role, whereas others may be less clear. It really comes down to how relevant your experience is in relation to the role that you are applying to, and other factors such as whether you have experience in project or people management already, or whether you'd prefer a role with all-round structured support and induction that a graduate scheme would provide. It might be worth approaching the company to see if a recruiter can advise how different role levels work in that particular organisation, but if you don't get a response in time, then apply to both experienced hire and graduate-level roles. It certainly can't hurt, and hopefully a recruiter will get in touch to explain the best route for you.

References

Burnett, B. and Evans, D. (2018) *Designing Your Life: How to Build a Well-Lived, Joyful Life.* London: Vintage.

Caterine, C. (2020) *Leaving Academia: A Practical Guide*. Princeton, NJ: Princeton University Press.

Elvidge, L., Spencely, C. and Williams, E. (2017) *What Every Postdoc Needs to Know.* London: New Scientific.

Kahn, S. and Ginther, D. (2017) 'The impact of postdoctoral training on early careers in biomedicine,' *Nature Biotechnology*, 35, pp. 90–94. doi: 10.1038/nbt.3766.

Wouterse, B., van der Wiel, K. and van der Steeg, M. (2017) 'Income Differences between PhDs and Masters: Evidence from The Netherlands,' *De Economist*, 165, pp. 439–446. doi: 10.1007/s10645-017-9304-9

5 Finding and forging opportunities beyond academia

In this chapter, we look at turning what you've learned so far into practical strategies for launching your career move beyond academia. This is the part of the process often referred to as 'job hunting,' but which we will explore as a more proactive process not just of finding, but also forging, opportunities: a process that you can (and should) set in motion well in advance of applying for jobs. Let's start, therefore, by considering what evidence tells us about how researchers land jobs in other sectors, and why these strategies might work.

What's the evidence?

You have to look long and hard to find published research specifically focused on how former doctoral and postdoctoral researchers successfully find, or create, their first/next roles beyond academia. However, the evidence that is out there suggests that contacts and networks play a significant role in helping researchers identify opportunities (Germain-Alamartine et al., 2021), including:

DOI: 10.4324/9781003589785-6

- Industrial partners or research sponsors.
- Contacts developed during the doctorate, either through members of academic faculty or through research partners or collaborators.
- Connections made before the doctorate, e.g. during previous degrees or jobs.
- In a small minority of cases, direct referrals from supervisors or managers.
- Links made at university events, e.g. events run by student associations featuring external guests.

A more recent study of PhD graduates in Australia also suggests that your contacts can be crucial, showing that those who found employment notably 'leveraged their social networks' to do so, including using personal connections to introduce them to prospective employers (Pham, 2025: 443). Seeking to address the dearth of published research in this area, online content creators have also launched their own initiatives to track researchers' career transitions, which reveal similar findings. By tracking 100 doctoral graduates for her website 'PhD Paths,' for instance, Ashley Moses (2024) found that the most common means through which they found jobs beyond academia were personal networks. Making up the remainder of the top five most successful job-hunting methods for Moses' sample were (from most to least popular): using LinkedIn; creating a position themselves (e.g. setting up their own businesses); finding openings on company websites; and using recruiters.

This prominence of networking and word-of-mouth channels makes sense when we look at general research on how employers hire. For example, in 2025, 61% of roles in large US firms were filled internally by existing employees, compared to just 28% in 2020 (The Daily Hire, 2025). The picture appears similar in Europe, where 66% of employers in the EU would 'most of the time' or 'always' begin the process of filling a vacancy by considering suitable internal candidates (Bertheau, 2021: 2). Indeed, hiring candidates who already work for (or with) their organisation, or have done so previously, presents several advantages for employers, saving time and money on firm-specific training and potentially motivating their workforce by demonstrating opportunities for progression (1–2). Furthermore, if you work in an organisation already, then you are more likely to be familiar with its structure and processes, and may have existing working relationships with colleagues that could be useful in the new role.

Inevitably, the prevalence of internal hiring varies according to the employment law of the country within which you are job hunting. However, in countries including the US and the UK there is technically no legal requirement for employers to advertise vacancies, hence evidence shows that as well as hiring internally, recruiting new staff via employers' own networks (and those of their employees) is also common in the Global North, through processes such as recommendations and referrals. This is where an employer may recruit to a vacancy by considering candidates who they have met previously, or who come recommended by existing employees and other contacts. Filling vacancies in this way also has potential benefits for employers, including:

- Referrals acting as a form of pre-screening, saving time assessing candidate quality (Davis et al., 2021).
- Smoother transition of recruits into the role due to existing social ties within their new workplace (Davis et al., 2021).

- Access to more information about a candidate's 'back story' (e.g. their past performance) than can be gleaned from a written application (Burks et al., 2013: 22).
- Candidates develop more accurate and realistic expectations about the job and the organisation through the referral process, increasing the likelihood that they will be satisfied in the role (Burks et al., 2013: 22).
- Avoiding costs involved in more formal screening and recruitment methods, such as using a recruitment agency (Gürtzgen and Pohlan, 2024).

Hiring new staff through existing contacts may significantly reduce the time and cost of recruitment. Some employers clearly capitalise upon this, with data from the US showing that around 40% of job candidates who come through referral progress to interview stage, compared to only 3% of candidates who apply through open channels without a prior relationship to the company (Ashby, 2025). Furthermore, the benefits of word-of-mouth hiring can be especially attractive to smaller organisations which are less likely to have the budget and the internal governance structures needed to run formalised recruitment processes (Bills et al., 2017: 300).[1]

Ways that employers might identify suitable candidates through these 'informal' means include asking current employees, placement students, and interns to recommend suitable candidates from their networks, with some companies even offering bonus payments to employees who refer a contact who is then successfully recruited (Pollard et al., 2015: 96). Professional and social networks can also act as sources of recommendations and referrals for hiring managers, including client companies or customers (Pollard et al., 2015: 96), as can 'contacts developed in work-related environments like professional associations, former jobs, conferences, etc.'

(Gerxhani and Koster, 2015: 786). With employers' networks playing such a key role in identifying potential candidates, relying solely on job boards to make your move beyond academia means potentially limiting your options, and that since

> A lot of jobs will end up being filled by somebody who knows somebody [...] if you just sit looking at internet ads for jobs, you are going to find it very tough... An awful lot is still done through recommendation...so you need to be networked.
>
> (Pollard et al., 2015: 97)

There are, nevertheless, potential equity issues for employers when filling vacancies in such informal ways. For example, evidence shows that candidates from minoritised ethnic backgrounds are more likely to experience disadvantage due to limited networks (e.g. Pedulla and Pager, 2019), and since people are more likely to refer others like themselves (e.g. similar age, ethnicity, and gender), hiring through existing contacts – especially current employees – means employers risk perpetuating a lack of diversity in their workforce (Kumar, 2025).

For researchers specifically, external exposure during doctoral or postdoctoral work is also an advantage, as landing a job, or having a role created for you, within a previous partner, sponsor, or collaborating company offers more direct routes into working beyond academia (Germain-Alamartine et al., 2021: 2685–2687). However, this also suggests that leveraging your networks to transition beyond academia is likely to be smoother if your research expertise closely matches the needs of such companies. If you come from a subject area with less 'obvious' applications in other sectors, or that is less likely to involve industry partnership at doctoral and postdoctoral level, you may therefore have to work harder to build your networks. Nevertheless, this isn't impossible; for example, research shows doctoral graduates from social sciences, arts, and humanities subjects undertaking other means of informal job-hunting such as building their networks through volunteering for community groups and NGOs, or securing an entry-level role within an organisation and using this to access internal opportunities and promotion (Guerin,2020: 319). Access to networks beyond academia may also depend on your location, as the amount of industry exposure typical during a doctorate and the likelihood of having work experience pre-doctorate varies between countries and cultures (e.g. Germain-Alamartine et al., 2021: 2687–2688). When it comes to filling vacancies through networks and word of mouth, employers therefore risk systematically favouring candidates with certain backgrounds and profiles.

Beyond hiring through their networks, employers use a range of other recruitment methods to fill openings within their organisations. For example, sector-specific channels such as trade publications, professional bodies, and employer organisations linked to relevant industries or disciplines can offer economical ways for employers to advertise vacancies to candidates with appropriate skills and expertise (Pollard et al., 2015: 95). Online marketing methods also act as cost-effective means of reaching potential candidates, from interactive activities like virtual tours of employers' premises, to placing more traditional online adverts on company websites and on both general and industry-specific job boards (94–95). On the other hand, advertising vacancies online may also attract high numbers of applications which can slow down the recruitment process, with recruiters in the UK reporting that hiring candidates through job adverts took on average 39% longer than sourcing candidates through their existing networks (JobAdder, 2024: 25). For many employers, reaching a wider pool of candidates by placing a vacancy on a job board comes with potential trade-offs including increased admin and longer recruitment times.

Furthermore, research shows that placing job advertisements does not necessarily overcome the equity issues that can arise with hiring internally or informally. In their well-known study of labour market discrimination, Bertrand and Mullainathan (2004) sent CVs (resumes) in response to over 1,300 job adverts placed in newspapers in Chicago and Boston and found that compared to candidates with African- American-sounding names, applicants with white-sounding names were 49% more likely to receive a callback in Chicago and 50% more likely to in Boston (998). Similar research also shows that individuals from minoritised ethnic backgrounds are less likely to be hired than those belonging to the majority population not only in the US, but also in the UK, Germany, The Netherlands, Norway, and Spain (Lancee, 2021),[2] whilst in Australia, a more recent study found that when applying for leadership positions, applicants with non-English names received 57.4% fewer positive responses than applicants with English names, and 45.3% fewer positive responses for non-leadership positions (Adamovic and Leibbrandt, 2023). Whilst placing job adverts may reach a wider pool of candidates, evidence nevertheless shows that discrimination still restricts some groups' access to opportunities.

What does this mean for you?

From the evidence summarised above, one key message stands out: *relying solely on job adverts limits your access to opportunities beyond academia.*

We have already seen some of the reasons for this, but a major factor here is **risk**. Recruitment can be costly for employers in terms of money, time, and other resources like training. When hiring you, therefore, an employer wants reassurance that if they offer you a role, you will perform well in it, enjoy it, will work effectively with your colleagues, and won't leave them having to go through the whole process again to replace you in a few months' time. Despite the drawbacks we have noted, hiring internally or through networks helps employers to feel they are reducing such risks by recruiting candidates who are already tried and trusted, vouched for, and who are more likely to transition smoothly into the organisation and role.

Appreciating the risks that recruitment poses for employers and factoring this into your job hunt is crucial. For example, many doctoral and postdoctoral researchers I work with think of job hunting as a passive 'call and answer process' in which an employer 'calls' with a job advert, and they 'answer' with an application. Instead, I encourage you to approach your job hunt as a set of conversations and interactions: a proactive, dynamic process in which you actively develop knowledge about the labour market, build trust with potential employers, and can access opportunities filled through a range of different recruitment methods. This is why the introduction to this book suggests starting on the actions in this chapter during the mid-stage of your doctorate or postdoc, rather than leaving them until the end. This kind of proactive job hunting is a *research process*: just as you wouldn't try to cram your fieldwork/experiments, data gathering, analysis, and write-up all into the last few months of your doctorate or postdoc, the same should apply to the research process of finding or forging your next opportunity beyond academia.

The most effective job-hunting methods are likely to differ depending on what you are seeking. As the case studies featured later in this chapter show, however, this doesn't always require having a specific job title in mind. In fact, several case study contributors based their job hunts on more general themes such as wanting to use certain skills, needing work in a specific location, or wanting to work towards a particular cause. Some openly acknowledge that their first roles beyond academia had job titles they hadn't even heard of before. Another benefit of approaching the job hunt as a proactive and interactive process, therefore, is that this allows you to uncover opportunities that you don't know the name of, or that may carry different names across different employers and sectors.

It helps to develop your interactive, 'mixed methods' job hunt based not solely on job titles but based on what you want your next role to give you according to your keep/lose/add profile from Chapter 2. Next, we look at how to tailor your job search according to this. The methods under each heading are neither exhaustive nor mutually exclusive, and you may decide to mix-and-match your chosen techniques according to what best fits with your priorities, preferences, and academic discipline. They are instead intended to offer a selection of starting points to prevent you from simply waiting around for algorithms to send the ideal role your way: small, actionable steps that you can (and, if possible, should) take well in advance of applying for roles.

'Keeping' or 'adding' specific skills, knowledge, or work activities

If your keep/lose/add profile revealed that there are certain skills you want to keep using in your work, methods to uncover relevant opportunities include:

- Talking to friends, former peers/colleagues, and other contacts with whom you have a high level of trust and whose jobs or workplaces are likely to involve using those skills. Even if their organisations don't currently have openings, letting them know that you are looking means they can reach out when opportunities arise. See Emma's story in case study 5.1 for an example of this in practice.
- Exploring opportunities with stakeholders. If your research has involved working with an industrial partner or other interested parties such as charities, companies, or public-sector bodies, use these to explore options. Find out more about the roles held by your direct contacts; alternatively, ask if they might be willing to connect you to any colleagues with backgrounds similar to yours, or working in teams and departments that might interest you. Seek opportunities such as presenting to your collaborating organisation(s) and talking to staff about their organisation's needs, to increase your chances of being considered for internal vacancies.
- If working for your immediate partner or sponsoring organisations is unlikely to involve using the skills you prefer, find out whether they have any client or partner organisations where this is more likely, and ask trusted contacts if they can introduce you.

- Make the most of conferences. Research in advance where relevant companies will be exhibiting and explore opportunities to present at conferences where you can show the potential impact of your skills and knowledge for organisations in attendance. Prepare a quick 'opener' that you can use to start a conversation based on what you know about their work and how this overlaps with your interests, and get contacts' details that you can use to follow up afterwards. See Alice's story in case study 5.3 for an example of this.
- Using less-than-ideal job vacancies to uncover more appropriate opportunities. When you come across adverts for roles that don't quite fit your preferences or experience level, but are based in organisations which could have other opportunities that might, use this to start a conversation. Find a named contact on the job advert or the person associated with the vacancy on LinkedIn, for example, and reach out to them. Explain your interest in their organisation and that you would like to discuss how the role may fit/not fit your experience and goals. I've seen numerous doctoral and postdoctoral researchers be referred to other more suitable openings through such conversations; see Nelly's story in case study 5.4 for an example.

Finding roles linked to a specific sector or 'mission'

If you're driven by working towards a particular 'mission' or cause, supporting a specific group of people, or contributing to a particular sector of the economy, then you could proactively identify opportunities by:

- Using LinkedIn or other appropriate platforms to follow relevant professionals. These could be people whose work makes the kind of difference that you want to make, who support people you want to support, or whose work involves creating products or solving problems to which you would like to contribute. If you do have example job titles in mind, then find and follow people already working in these roles. This will then bring any job postings that these people share into your feeds; see Showforth's story in case study 5.2 below for an example of this.
- Performing a LinkedIn 'people search' to identify where former research students and/or staff from your institution are working now. Search for your current or most recent university or research institute in the LinkedIn search bar and select 'people' in the menu bar. Then, select 'all filters.' Scroll down to find 'past company' and tick your institution, then scroll down again to find 'industry' and select a sector that interests you. This will display people who used to be based at your institution but who now work in this sector. To find out specifically where the former doctoral or postdoctoral researchers are, look in the 'past' section of their profile thumbnail for those whose former role was Doctoral Researcher, Research Fellow, or whatever terms tend to be used for such positions in your country. Looking at what these people do now and where they work could help you to identify roles and potential employers linked to your mission or sector of interest, that you could focus on in your job hunt.
- Looking up which companies or organisations are involved in writing technical white papers, sit on expert panels, contribute to standards or guidelines,

or sponsor or attend conferences in your sector or area of interest are other ways to identify potential employers.

- Using sector-specific job boards and resources which can make your job hunt more targeted. An online search for terms such as 'sector-specific job board charities' or 'sector-specific job board pharmaceuticals' should help you to identify potential resources.
- Using recruitment agencies, if these operate in your target country. Search online for 'recruitment agency + sector,' for example 'recruitment agency life sciences' or 'recruitment agency public sector' to identify recruiters who specialise in filling vacancies for employers in your sector(s) of interest.
- Volunteering. This of course depends on your capacity to undertake unpaid work, but could offer access to internal opportunities. For example, completing training as a volunteer for a sight loss charity in the UK gave one doctoral researcher access to the charity's internal-only job board. Taking on voluntary roles can also give insights into how organisations work, which could be useful for job applications further down the line.

Finding roles in a specific organisation of interest

If you have identified specific companies or types of organisations you would like to work for, some ways to uncover opportunities include:

- Creating a Google Alert for the company's name and the word 'jobs' or 'vacancies' to get new postings sent your way. Alternatively, some organisations may allow you to create an account and to set your preferences to be emailed when relevant opportunities are advertised.

- Exploring part-time work with an organisation of interest alongside your doctorate could lead to further opportunities. Another route could be initially moving into a position closely linked to your research as a 'way in' to the organisation or starting with an entry-level role, to then gain exposure to internal opportunities.
- Undertaking an internship, placement, or external secondment or fellowship. Such opportunities may be 'built into' your doctorate, may be negotiable during your programme or current contract, or may even be available through your university's career service or similar department. They can be used not only to gain experience, but also to build a network within an organisation and uncover potential internal openings.
- Following up with people based in your organisation(s) of interest who have posted about job openings that don't quite fit your preferences or experience level. Job adverts can be an indication that a team or organisation has recently received funding or is expanding: reach out to the person advertising, explain your interest and what you have to offer, and ask if any of their colleagues may have more appropriate opportunities available.
- Researching whether your preferred organisation will be attending any events such as careers fairs or industry conferences and arranging to go along. Prepare a conversation starter based on what you know about them and how their work overlaps with your skills and expertise and get contact details that you can use to follow up afterwards.

Finding roles in a specific location

If staying in, or moving to, a particular region or country is important in your job search, then using the 'location' function on job boards might be the most obvious way of finding job openings within your desired radius. Other more proactive ways to identify potential opportunities include:

- Talking to current trusted contacts to see if they know people working in your preferred location(s) who may be able to recommend relevant job-hunting resources.
- Using the LinkedIn alumni search (see Chapter 3) to identify companies around which to target your search. Search alumni of your current or previous university according to 'where they live' and 'what they do' or 'what they are skilled at' to identify organisations in your chosen location that may offer roles relevant to your interests. You could also apply the same searches using the alumni sections of universities based in your target location.
- Researching whether there are country-specific platforms that are used for job hunting in your target location(s) and sign up to these. This includes creating a presence on the go-to professional social networking site for your target country (which may be different from the ones used in your current location).
- Using the tips above to identify and follow/connect with people who:
  - Work in recruitment and talent acquisition for organisations in your target location, so that when they post about any openings these will show up in your feed.
  - Have made the same country move that you are hoping to make. Looking where these people work

can help you to identify potential employers in your target area, or who are open to recruiting international candidates. Using the 'where they live' filter in the LinkedIn alumni search can be useful to identify such individuals; see the 'What does this mean for you?' section of Chapter 3 for details on how to find and use this function.

Before acting on these (or any other) tips, however, understanding professional etiquette in your target location(s) is crucial. If you plan to job hunt in a country where you haven't worked before, don't assume that the unspoken rules around what you can expect from your network are the same as in your home or previous countries. In some cultures, for example, the initiative shown by researching potential employers or reaching out to people beyond your network may be considered undesirable; equally, some cultures may consider asking people questions about their jobs and employers to be an invasion of privacy or an indication of disloyalty (Goodman et al., 1988: 58–59). Understanding such dynamics in the culture of your target locations is therefore crucial preparation for your job hunt, to avoid deterring potential employers and to ensure that you are not conducting your job hunt based on flawed cultural assumptions or stereotypes. Talking to alumni or former employees of your university or research institute who have already made a move to your target country is also a useful starting point for this.

Creating a role for yourself

We've seen how creating their own role was the third most common way in which doctoral graduates tracked by Moses (2024) shifted into other sectors. Some ways to carve out such opportunities include:

- Reaching out to people who are likely to understand the needs and gaps within their organisation that your skills and knowledge could fill. This could involve contacting hiring managers who are currently recruiting to roles in organisations linked to your skills and expertise by requesting an informal discussion about the vacancy. This could also involve researching and approaching small, specialist organisations like spin-out companies where your expertise may be in demand. In the UK for example the 'HESA Spin Out Register' offers an official list of all spin-out companies produced by UK universities that you can search according to location and subject area.
- Using your expertise (including methods or findings from your research) to inform or upskill other professionals or populations. Consider whose professional practice could be enhanced through your insights and how you could reach these people, be it through training, professional development publications, professional associations, or otherwise. See Showforth's story in case study 5.2 for an example.
- Creating opportunities through consulting. This means identifying groups or individuals who might be facing problems that your expertise could help to solve (your clients) and devising strategies to reach them and offer your services. Ways to kick-start this during your doctoral research could be using your research findings to advise external organisations or seeking opportunities to undertake projects that use your research for

external impact; your current institution may have an enterprise, innovation, or knowledge transfer office who could advise. See Alice's story in case study 5.3 for an example.

Addressing limited networks and equity issues

With so many career opportunities uncovered via informal, word-of-mouth channels, you may feel disadvantaged if you are not currently connected to people working in sectors, roles, or locations that may interest you. Equally, you may not feel adequately represented in relevant career areas or may feel isolated from others who are looking to make similar career transitions.

If this is the case, identifying existing networks or groups that unite people with interests or backgrounds similar to yours could help you find solidarity. This could include:

- Joining free networks or groups focused on helping academics transition into other sectors or start your own. See Gabrielle's case study in Chapter 1 for an example of this.
- Joining networks that support and connect professionals with protected characteristics, such as BYP Network (a UK network focused on advancing the careers of black professionals), oSTEM (an international non-profit society focused on LGBTQ+ people in STEM), and WHEN (Women's Higher Education Network). Your current institution may have its own networks

dedicated (for example) to disabled staff, LGBTQIA+ staff, and other protected characteristics, that could introduce you to new contacts and allies.

- Accessing job boards and careers resources that promote the professional prospects of people with protected characteristics, such as Evenbreak (focused on inclusive jobs for people with disabilities or long-term health conditions), Vericada, and BME jobs.
- Using job platforms designed for international students. In the UK for instance, Student Circus is one example of a job board that focuses on advertising roles with companies who sponsor appropriate work visas for international applicants. The careers service at your current institution may have subscriptions to such platforms, allowing you to access them for free.

Get to work

Now we've spent some time understanding how employers hire and how to access openings filled through a range of recruitment methods, we next turn to practical exercises to help you apply what you've learned so far to finding and forging opportunities beyond academia.

Exercise 5.1: Adapting your current job-hunting methods

To switch up your job search, start by reviewing job-hunting techniques you are considering or are already using, that you have used in the past, or that people you know have used. Use a grid like Table 5.1 to list these, along with the level of risk involved for the employer to

Table 5.1 Reviewing current job-hunting methods according to risk for the employer

Job hunting method	*Risks for employers*	*How to reduce risk for employers*
Using LinkedIn 'easy apply': information for your application is pulled from your profile.	• Risk of high number of applications, many of which may be irrelevant • Risk that applications received in this way do not feed through automatically to an organisation's recruitment system. • Risk of needing lots of time to shortlist.	Look up the employer's vacancy website to see if you can apply via there instead, if this will give you the option to submit a more tailored application (e.g. cover letter).
Finding a job advert and applying online.	• Risk of high number of applications, many of which may not be tailored to the role. • Risk of needing lots of time to shortlist. • Risk of hiring someone who is 'unknown' to the company.	Contacting the person advertising the role (or person named on the advert) for an informal discussion about the role to highlight your interest and build a rapport. Ask them questions that will help you to tailor your application, e.g. why the role came up, and if it is attached to any particular goals the organisation wants to achieve.

recruit in this way. Use what we learned above about the pros and cons of different hiring methods to help you. Then, in the final column, think about how you could adapt each method to reduce the level of risk to the employer, and to increase their trust in you as a candidate. Table 5.1 gives some examples to get you started.

We've seen that recruitment methods also pose potential risks for you as a candidate, including risks around whether a particular organisation is a good fit for you, or issues of inequity and discrimination raised by the use of certain recruitment and shortlisting practices.

Create a table listing job hunting methods you might use, and the risks involved for you in finding or forging opportunities in these ways. Use what we learned above about the pros and cons of different hiring methods to help you. Then, in the final column, think about whether there is anything you can do to mitigate these risks, or to establish your rights in the hiring process. Table 5.2 gives some examples.

Exercise 5.2: Activating your network

Some of the job-hunting activities outlined in this chapter may seem daunting, especially if you feel uncomfortable or inexperienced with networking. The crucial thing to remember is that the practices to which we usually refer to as 'networking' are primarily based on **trust.** What you can reasonably expect from anyone in your network depends on the level of trust you have built with them, and how confident they are that your actions will preserve their reputation. For example, a doctoral graduate with whom you have recently connected on LinkedIn might be happy to point you to a job board or recruitment agency that helped

Table 5.2 Reviewing job-hunting methods according to risks for you as a candidate

Job hunting method	*Risks for you*	*How to reduce risk*
Finding a job advert and applying online.	• Risk of discrimination because my name isn't typical of the majority population in my country. • I haven't worked at an organisation like this before: how do I know I'll like it? • Job hunt taking longer due to employers receiving higher volumes of applications due to factors such as layoffs and applicants' use of generative AI.	Know where to find guidance if I think a job advert is discriminatory, or if I experience discrimination in the recruitment process. E.g. in the UK, contact the Advisory, Conciliation and Arbitration Service (ACAS) helpline and look up guidance from the Equality and Human Rights Commission, or look up your country's equivalent. Research organisations to which I'm applying to see if they have a diverse workforce and management team. Use the LinkedIn tips in Chapter 3 to reach out to alumni from my university who work at the organisation to see if they'd be happy to talk. Prepare questions to ask in the interview to gauge whether this organisation is a good fit for me. Build a financial buffer (e.g. savings to cover living costs) to support myself if job hunting takes longer than hoped.

(*Continued*)

Table 5.2 (Continued)

Job hunting method	*Risks for you*	*How to reduce risk*
Accessing opportunities through 'word of mouth'	• I have been a carer during my PhD and haven't been able to attend many networking events or careers events on campus, so I have a limited network to draw on.	Joining a free group focused on helping academics transition into other sectors, like those listed at the end of Chapter 1; introduce myself in a post or at a virtual meeting. Use LinkedIn to connect with people who have spoken at events that I have missed, to see if they would be happy to answer some questions about their organisation and how they found their jobs.

them to find their current role. However, such a contact is unlikely to feel they have enough knowledge about you and your skills, and hence enough trust in you, to directly recommend you for a vacancy in their company. Taking stock of your current network, therefore, can help to both make your mixed-methods job hunt less intimidating by starting with people you already know, and can help you to understand how you can (and can't) leverage your existing network to find opportunities beyond academia.

Use Table 5.3 to map your current network and to devise ways to build this. The activities in the left-hand column of the table require increasing amounts of trust. Write down anyone with whom you have an appropriate amount of trust who could help you with any of these activities now, or who might be able to if you were to develop your relationship. In the far left-hand column, use the research and tips covered above to devise ways to grow your network to include people who may be able to help you with some of these things. In the activity descriptions, the word 'relevant' could mean related to your preferred knowledge and skills, in your preferred location(s), working in your preferred organisations, and so-on.

Case study

Case studies 5.1–5.4 show examples of how real researchers found and forged opportunities beyond academia. When reading the case studies, note the actions that each researcher took that led them to landing their first role beyond academia. Even if they don't have the same subject background as you, consider how you could adapt and apply some of their job-hunting methods to your own search.

Table 5.3 Mapping and growing your current network

	Can do this for you now	*Could do this for you if you develop the relationship*	*Ways to find people you don't know yet who could do this*
Share adverts for, or announcements about, relevant opportunities on LinkedIn/social media that you could see in your feed			
Point you towards adverts for relevant posts, or towards places where these may be advertised (e.g. sector-specific job boards)			
Recommend a recruiter or employment agency that helped them find a job in your target sector or location			
Have a chat with you about their company or organisation, to make a good impression for any current or future opportunities			

(*Continued*)

Table 5.3 (Continued)

	Can do this for you now	*Could do this for you if you develop the relationship*	*Ways to find people you don't know yet who could do this*
Refer you to any of their contacts for a chat about their company or organisation(s), for you to build a relationship and potentially be informed of future opportunities			
Directly recommend you for a job in their current organisation, or in an organisation with which they have connections			
Offer you a job in their company or organisation			
Offer you freelance or contracting work based on your skills and their needs			

Case study 5.1 Emma (PhD in Biochemical Engineering)

Finding opportunities through friends

In the final year of my PhD, I knew I wanted to move away from research and into a career that focused on communicating complex concepts, working across different scientific and healthcare disciplines, and solving interdisciplinary problems. However, I had no idea where to begin searching for a role that encompassed those things! I decided to speak to a friend of mine who had done a PhD in a similar field and who now worked for a company that made scientific instruments. She told me that they were looking for someone to fill a role called a Field Application Specialist to work within their physical sciences division. At the time I had never heard of this role before, but I was excited to learn from my friend that it would combine a deep knowledge of the company's scientific products with an understanding of scientists' needs and how each product could provide a solution for their challenges. I knew this would involve using the kinds of skills I enjoyed most so I applied for the job, got it, and have since progressed throughout my career from Marketing Manager to Senior Product Marketing Executive, and now I am Product Lead for a medical device company. Who knows, if I had never spoken to my friend, I may have never found that first opportunity!

Case study 5.2 Showforth (PhD and two postdocs in Microbiology)

Forging opportunities through networking

My first job hunt beyond academia was in the UK. I have a passion for helping researchers navigate their careers, so I followed practitioners and leaders in this field on LinkedIn. One of them posted a vacancy for a Research Culture Specialist on LinkedIn, which involved work that I had been doing 'on the side' for free for many years. I applied and was offered the job. The role and the team suited me well; however, life happened! My wife needed to go and work outside the UK, so I had to resign and move to Ghana.

In Ghana, my job-hunting experience has so far been very different. It is a relatively small country and is currently experiencing economic hardship, meaning there are fewer career opportunities beyond academia than there are in the UK. Remuneration is also much lower. There is also currently a government embargo on employment by public universities. I have tried to secure academic and non-academic roles, but none of these have materialised yet. So, in the meantime, I thought 'if nothing is available out there, why not create something for yourself?'

To job hunt, therefore, I have focused on building and leveraging my networks. For example, I reached out to organisers of a writing workshop for African researchers and was invited to co-facilitate sessions on writing manuscripts and funding applications. I am also Co-Chair of a microbiology network in Nigeria where I ran several capacity-building workshops for researchers, which then led to an invitation to run workshops for new PhD students at a university in South Africa. Plus, my understanding of the European research funding landscape has also helped me build links with some organisations with whom I am currently discussing potential collaborations. Building and leveraging my networks in this way has allowed me to continue supporting researchers and develop my experience in doing so.

Case study 5.3 Alice (PhD History)

Forging opportunities through conferences

My doctoral research examined Anglican missionaries' involvement in transatlantic slavery in the early 19th century. During my PhD, I applied for some funding from my university to run a pilot project on 'contested heritage' in local churches, as I was interested in the physical legacies of enslavement and colonialism. I spoke about the project at one of the Church's annual conferences where I met some people who told me about an opportunity to submit a bid (often called a 'tender' outside of academia) for some freelance work for the Church around contested heritage. I submitted a successful tender for the work around the time I was awarded my PhD, and a year later I'm still offering freelance consultancy to the same division.

This was also a way to continue work that I started in my PhD. Something that I wasn't expecting to have to consider post-PhD was that it doesn't always feel 'right' to completely leave your research behind. I had built so many connections with (and gotten so much from) the churches I had worked with that I wanted to continue supporting them, which ultimately led to longer-term work. If you do want to stay working in your field (but not necessarily in academia) as I did, try to stay active in your networks and attend conferences if you can: some offer concessions or grants for those considered to be 'early career.' This keeps you up-to-date and helps you meet people who might be interested in your skills and experience. Personally, I have found that academics are keen to hear from practical experiences 'in industry.' Also, setting up an email address and a basic website with information about your work and contact details allows people to get in touch with you about your expertise. Plus, if you aren't attached to a university anymore then people still have something to read when they Google you!

Case study 5.4 Nelly (PhD Modern Greek Studies)

Finding opportunities through talking to hiring managers

After my PhD, I went to work for a firm that undertakes policy-related research and evaluation projects for public-sector clients (e.g. government departments) and charities. Before securing this job though, I didn't really understand what public-sector consulting or working in research and evaluation entailed.

My journey into that first role started when I saw a copywriting role with the company advertised online. Having done a humanities doctorate, I felt confident about my ability to do a writing-focused role, so initially I reached out and enquired about this position. After an informal chat, however, the managing director – who also hired me – encouraged me that I could define my own role in the company (which as a start-up then offered that level of flexibility) and instead persuaded me to consider going for a research manager role. Previously, I hadn't realised this was an option; the company's name made me assume that it focused on management or financial consulting, which wouldn't suit my qualitative skills or my humanities PhD.

Once I started in the research manager role, it became clear that I had lots of relevant skills beyond writing, particularly in research, analysis, and bid writing. In academia, this would be equivalent to grant writing or drafting funding applications: essentially, securing funding to conduct research. I realised that these skills translated well into the business world, where research and business development (winning new work) are closely linked. Over time, I began contributing to both research projects and proposal writing. I only fully recognised that I was capable of doing the job after experiencing it firsthand. The work wasn't fundamentally different from what I had done before, but I had to repurpose my skills, adapting to a faster working pace and more business-focused language.

Takeaways

- Evidence shows that many doctoral and postdoctoral researchers find their first roles beyond academia through contacts and networks.
- Focusing your job hunt solely on responding to job adverts means that you are likely to miss a significant number of vacancies that are filled through informal 'word of mouth' channels.
- Job hunting doesn't have to mean searching for specific job titles; instead, you can design a mixed-methods approach to find and forge opportunities that align with your priorities.
- Recruitment carries risks for employers, who want to be confident that new hires can do the job well, will enjoy the job, and will not leave them needing to re-recruit in a few months' time.
- Reduce perceived risk for employers by building relationships early, for example through pre-application discussions with hiring managers or conversations at events and conferences. Be aware of potential equity issues with employers' hiring methods; know where to go to understand your rights and use relevant groups and communities to seek solidarity.

- To make networking less daunting, start by mapping your current network and talking to people you already know. See if existing contacts may know people it may be useful to chat to, given your interests and priorities.
- Conduct your mixed-methods job hunt according to appropriate etiquette. This includes leveraging your contacts sensitively according to your level of trust and taking time to understand the customs in your target region or country.
- Treat job hunting as a proactive process built through conversations and interactions.

Notes

1 Depending on the country in which you are job hunting, the feasibility of using recommendations and referrals to fill vacancies may vary between different types and sizes of organisations. For example, greater public visibility and accountability often means that public sector organisations are less likely than those in the private sector to use the kinds of informal recruitment methods (Bills et al., 2017: 300).

2 Evidence also shows that the most discriminated against groups in recruitment processes vary depending on the country in question (e.g. Ramos *et al.*, 2021; Thijssen et al., 2021).

References

Adamovic, M. and Leibbrandt, A. (2023) 'Is there a glass ceiling for ethnic minorities to enter leadership positions?', *The Leadership Quarterly*, 34(2), pp. 1–13. doi: 10.1016/j.leaqua.2022.101655.

Ashby (2025) *Referrals in Hiring: Talent Trends Report*. Available at: https://www.ashbyhq.com/talent-trends-report/reports/referrals [Accessed 13 December 2025]

Bertheau, A. (2021) 'Employer search behavior: reasons for internal hiring,' *Labour Economics*, 73, 102064. doi: 10.1016/j.labeco.2021.102064.

Bertrand, M. and Mullainathan, S. (2004) 'Are Emily and Greg more employable than Lakisha and Jamal? A field experiment on labor market discrimination,' *American Economic Review*, 94(4), pp. 991–1013. doi: 10.1257/0002828042002561.

Bills, D., Di Stasio, V. and Gërxhani, K. (2017) 'The demand side of hiring: employers in the labor market,' *Annual Review of Sociology*, 43, pp. 291–310. doi: 10.1146/annurev-soc-081715-074255.

Burks, S., Cowgill, B., Hoffman, M. and Housman, M. (2013) '"You'd be perfect for this:" understanding the value of hiring through referrals,' *IZA Discussion Paper Series*, No. 7382. Available at: https://docs.iza.org/dp7382.pdf

Davis, S.J., Macaluso, C. and Waddell, S.R. (2021) 'How do employers recruit new workers?', *Richmond Fed Economic Brief*, 21(28). Available at: https://www.richmondfed.org/publications/research/economic_brief/2021/eb_21-28 [Accessed 13 December 2025]

Germain-Alamartine, E., Ahoba-Sam, R., Moghadam-Saman, S. and Evers, G. (2021) 'Doctoral graduates' transition to industry: networks as a mechanism? Cases from Norway, Sweden and the UK,' *Studies in Higher Education*, 46(12), pp. 2680–2695. doi: 10.1080/03075079.2020.1754783.

Gerxhani, K. and Koster, F. (2015) 'Making the right move: investigating employers' recruitment strategies,' *Personnel Review*, 44, pp. 781–800. doi: 10.1108/PR-12-2013-0229

Goodman, A.P., Hartt, J.A., Pennington, M.K. and Terrell, K.P. (1988) 'International students and the job search,' *Journal of Career Planning and Employment*, 48(4), pp. 55–61.

Guerin, C. (2020) 'Stories of moving on: HASS PhD graduates' motivations and career trajectories inside and beyond academia,' *Arts and Humanities in Higher Education*, 19(3), pp. 304–324. doi: 10.1177/1474022219834448

Gürtzgen, N. and Pohlan, L. (2024) 'Do employers learn more from referrals than from other recruitment channels?', *Labour Economics*, 89. doi: 10.1016/j.labeco.2024.102574.

JobAdder (2024) *State of the market: ANZ & UK recruitment report Q1–Q2 2024*. Available at: https://jobadder.com/gb/resource/recruitment-report-state-of-the-market-h1-2024/

Kumar, N.R. (2025) 'A comparative effectiveness of 'employee referrals' vs 'traditional recruitment' methods in talent acquisition,' *International Journal of Research in Management*, 7(1), pp. 216–233. doi: 10.33545/26648792.2025.v7.i1c.283.

Lancee, B. (2021) 'Ethnic discrimination in hiring: comparing groups across contexts. Results from a cross-national field experiment,'

Journal of Ethnic and Migration Studies, 47(6), pp. 1181–1200. doi: 10.1080/1369183X.2019.1622744.

Moses, A. (2024) '100 PhDs left academia, and here's how they found their jobs.' [LinkedIn post] 17 December. Available at: https://www.linkedin.com/posts/ashley-moses-98a3m_100-phds-left-academia-and-heres-how-they-activity-7274800520991571968-IXOU [Accessed 2 February 2025].

Pedulla, D.S. and Pager, D. (2019) 'Race and networks in the job search process,' *American Sociological Review*, 84(6), pp. 983–1012. doi: 10.1177/0003122419883255.

Pham, T. (2025) 'What really contributes to employability of PhD graduates in uncertain labour markets?', *Globalisation, Societies and Education*, 23(2), pp. 435–446. doi: 10.1080/14767724.2023.2192908.

Pollard, E., Hirsh, W., Williams, M., Buzzeo, J., Marvell, R., Tassinari, A., Bertram, C., Fletcher, L., Artess, J., Redman, J. and Ball, C. (2015) *Understanding Employers' Graduate Recruitment and Selection Practices*. BIS Research Paper no. 231. Available at: https://www.gov.uk/government/publications/employers-graduate-recruitment-and-selection-practices [Accessed 2 February 2025].

Ramos, G., Delgadillo, D., Fossum, J., Montoya, A.K., Thamrin, H., Rapp, A., Escovar, A. and Chavira, D.A. (2021) 'Discrimination and internalizing symptoms in rural Latinx adolescents: An ecological model of etiology', *Children and Youth Services Review*, 130, p. 106250. doi: 10.1016/j.childyouth.2021.106250.

The Daily Hire (2025) *Internal Mobility Replacing External Hiring at Fortune 500.* Available at: https://thedailyhire.com/news/internal-mobility-programs-replacing-external-hiring-fortune-500 [Accessed 13 December 2025].

Thijssen, L., Coenders, M. and Lancee, B. (2021) 'Ethnic discrimination in the Dutch labor market: Differences between ethnic minority groups and the role of personal information about job applicants—evidence from a field experiment', *Journal of International Migration and Integration*, 22(3), pp. 1125–1150. doi: 10.1007/s12134-020-00795-w.

6 Communicating your value to employers beyond academia

Whether you access opportunities beyond academia through formal or informal channels, it's likely that you will need to navigate some kind of recruitment process, or at least convey your motivation, skills, and experience to potential employers, clients, or collaborators. Learning to convey the value that you bring to audiences beyond academia is crucial but can take practice, especially if the language of academia or of your former career area has become your 'default.'

From my own job hunt towards the end of my PhD, I distinctly remember feedback from one interview for a job in the arts and cultural sector, saying that I came across 'too academic,' that they questioned whether I wanted the role due to my 'previous experience and ambitions,' and that they felt others had shown 'more working knowledge and experience for this particular role.' My first response was confusion: I thought I'd come across as knowledgeable and enthusiastic, so was at a loss as to why the panel hadn't got that impression. To begin this chapter then, and to help you to avoid the pitfalls I fell into, we will look at research that examines common challenges in articulating your skills to employers when moving from academia. We'll look at studies presenting the perspectives of both

DOI: 10.4324/9781003589785-7

researchers and employers, identify potential conflicts in these perspectives, and then use this to explore what you can do to navigate potential stumbling blocks in recruitment processes.

This chapter isn't going to be filled with CV or resume templates for you to regurgitate in your job hunt, nor does it outline how to craft perfect answers to specific interview questions. Instead, it offers a framework for effectively articulating your skills, motivation, and value in ways that directly address common challenges faced by doctoral and postdoctoral researchers, be it in written applications, informal chats, or formal interviews. If CV/resume templates and detailed breakdowns of the interview process are what you're after, there are plenty of other resources out there that already cover this, including:

- Matteo Tardelli (2023). Beyond Academia: Stories and Strategies for PhDs Making the Leap to Industry.
- Isaiah Hankel (2023). *The Power of a PhD: How Anyone Can Use Their PhD to Get Hired in Industry.* New York: Morgan James.
- Tina Persson (ed.) (2025). *Job Hunting for the 21st Century: A Comprehensive Guide for the Modern PhD.* Cambridge: Royal Society of Chemistry.

In some job markets (e.g. the US), 'CV' refers to a longer, detailed document usually used for academic positions, whilst 'resume' is the term used for a shorter, more tailored document used for positions beyond academia. In the rest of this chapter, however, the term 'CV' is used throughout in the UK sense to refer to a concise, tailored document equivalent to a US resume.

What's the evidence?

When transitioning your career beyond academia, one of the most common challenges comes in articulating and 'quantifying' your academic experience in ways that resonate with employers and show your ability to work in more commercial environments (Boyd and McAlinden, 2016: 17–18). Indeed, some studies go so far as to suggest that for some, having a doctorate may even prove problematic during the job hunt, especially when applying for entry level roles, other roles that do not require a higher degree, or when returning to work after taking time out (e.g. Diamond et al. 2014: 54). Hence, despite it being good practice to use doctoral and postdoctoral experience to show skills and achievements relevant to the role, concerns around employers' perceptions can lead to candidates 'down-playing' their doctorate or even omitting it from their CV for fear of being perceived as 'too educated,' or even as 'a threat' (Suomi et al., 2020: 404).

If we consider employers' perspectives, it's easy to feel that such fears are justified. In the UK for example, evidence suggests that around 70% of employers find 'inability to market skills' to be a common issue when recruiting doctoral graduates (CIHE, 2010: 11). Lack of commercial awareness, overspecialisation, unrealistic expectations, and difficulty in adapting to non-academic work environments are also identified as drawbacks for employers when hiring doctorate holders (CIHE, 2010: 11), alongside deficiencies in interpersonal skills (e.g. Rubio and Hooley, 2010). Research also shows evidence of similar perceptions towards postdoctoral researchers, with employers citing issues including a lack of teamwork and leadership experience, as well as limited abilities 'to work under strict deadlines and budgets, cancel projects that do not yield results within a specific period, make brief pitches, and communicate complex concepts to non-scientific audiences' (Hayter and Parker, 2019: 563). Such perceptions help to explain why employers might also assume that candidates with doctoral or postdoctoral experience are likely to be overqualified for, and lack interest in, the work they offer, assuming that they 'would have only narrow knowledge or interest in their specialised area, have little real-world experience, or be socially inept' (Diamond et al., 2014: 72). Convincing employers beyond academia of your genuine interest in the opportunities they offer is therefore crucial, to show that you are intentionally shifting your career towards them rather than simply trying to escape academia or find a 'stop gap' (Peacey and Romijn, 2026).

The extent to which an employer understands the skills gained from academic research may further influence their attitudes. For instance, evidence shows that employers in sectors beyond academia can sometimes struggle to grasp what candidates with doctoral experience can offer over those with a Master's degree (Suomi et al., 2020: 410), or what value postdoctoral experience might add over and above completing a doctorate. The more experience an employer has of hiring doctorate holders, however, the higher they are likely to rate doctoral graduates' competence across a range of key skills including project management, interpersonal skills, and leadership (Rubio and Hooley, 2010). It comes as little surprise, therefore, that research shows a 'cumulative effect' in which organisations with a previous record of employing doctorate holders are more likely to hire more in the future (Garcia-Quevedo et al., 2012: 618).

If you have limited experience of talking about your skills to non-academic audiences, some of whom lack awareness of what doctoral or postdoctoral research actually entails, then knowing how to 'sell yourself' convincingly can be challenging, especially given that academia and other sectors often (literally) speak very different languages. For example, whilst both academics and other-sector employers sometimes use the same skill words (e.g. 'project management'), they may in fact refer to slightly different practices or activities when doing so, and hence speak with cross purposes (Muurlink et al., 2024: 961). Evidence also suggests a mismatch between the skills that researchers tend to assume are most important for working beyond academia (research skills and technical knowledge), and those most valued amongst employers (teamwork and collaboration) (959). As a researcher, what may feel most intuitive for you to focus on in job applications and interviews may therefore be at odds with an employer's priorities. This could, in turn, reinforce employers' perceptions that whilst academically smart, researchers lack the broader skills required to work effectively in other sectors.

However, the research isn't all doom and gloom. The evidence we've considered above also offers useful pointers for mitigating challenges around skill articulation, employers' perceptions, and avoiding misunderstandings during recruitment processes. Our next focus, then, is to synthesise the findings above into practical tips to make sure that your applications and interviews for jobs beyond academia really hit the mark.

What does this mean for you?

One key message that emerges from the evidence above is how important it is to speak the same language as an employer when applying for jobs beyond academia. If you can recognise what an employer really needs, and convince them that you can deliver that, then you can communicate with them on their terms, leaving less space for miscommunication and judgement. Before you can prepare truly effective applications and interviews for roles beyond academia, therefore, you need to:

1. Understand an employer's goals and problems.
2. Recognise your 'default settings,' i.e. how you tend to present yourself.
3. Recalibrate if there's a mismatch between 1 and 2.

Understanding an employer's goals or problems

When job adverts are vague or laden with jargon, it can be difficult to decipher what employers really want. Ultimately, however, any job vacancy that arises does so because a company or organisation wants to achieve a certain goal or solve a specific set of problems. In a job application, interview, or chat with a hiring manager, you need to show how you can help them to achieve those goals and/or solve those problems. Whether it's increasing sales, engaging wider audiences, launching new products, supporting certain groups of people, or whatever: showing how you can contribute to these goals, and thus to the success of the organisation, helps you not only to demonstrate your skills, but also to display the commercial awareness so often sought by employers beyond academia.

In the studies outlined above, employers' reservations around researchers' abilities to work collaboratively, to meet strict deadlines and budgets, to make difficult decisions (and so on) demonstrate scepticism as to whether someone moving from academia *would be able to help them solve their problems*. Communicating this clearly is one way of alleviating employers' potential doubts. To do this, it's crucial to understand the goals you'd be expected to help an employer to achieve, or what problems you'd be expected to help them solve, if you were appointed. Exercise 6.1 below is designed to help you with this.

Recognising your default settings

As well as seeing things from the employer's point of view, it's also important to reflect on how you are used to talking about yourself. For example, over-focusing on technical details about your research when an employer has other priorities risks alienating your audience, which is where impressions of being 'too smart,' too niche, and lacking interest in the employer's business may creep in.

My own interview feedback outlined earlier gives a glimpse of my default settings towards the end of my PhD. For example, when a panel member asked me a question about what equality meant to me, I gave a detailed answer referring to Henri Tajfel's social identity theory: I was so used to talking about critical and sociological theory in my academic life, that this is what automatically came out of my mouth at interview. The role I was interviewing for, however, was focused on customer service. A more appropriate answer, therefore, would have addressed what I felt equality meant when dealing with customers: in other words, I should have related my answer to the employer's goals and problems.

The same goes if you have work experience from before your doctorate but are now looking to make a career change. If employers in your new field have different problems or want to achieve different things than your previous employers did, then it's likely you will have to present yourself slightly differently to resonate with your new audience. Either way, recognising your current default settings and comparing these with the settings of your potential employers will help to mitigate issues such as being seen as 'too academic' or as lacking the skills required in other sectors.

Recalibrating

Once you've worked out what you'd be helping the employer to achieve or solve if you were hired into a particular role, and you've reflected on how you present yourself, your next task is to bring these two things into alignment by framing your skills and experience *in the context of the job or opportunity for which you are applying.*

In his book *Leaving Academia,* Chris Caterine (2020) describes this process of contextualisation well. Caterine explains that, as someone with academic teaching experience (for example), you might assume you'd be a good fit for an employer looking for someone with 'great communication skills'; however, 'unless you know what that phrase means in the context of the organisation, you're likely to miss the mark when enumerating your specific talents' (Caterine, 2020: 118). Recalibrating therefore means focusing your applications and interviews not just on showing communication skills, presentation skills, organisational skills (and so on) *in general*, but on choosing examples that best show that you can communicate, present, organise, etc. *in the way you'd need to do those things in the role(s) for which you are applying.* This means not simply assuming your skills are immediately transferable, but understanding how to frame them according to your target employer's 'value system' (Chen et al., 2026: 12).

Many researchers ask me, for example, whether a doctorate 'counts as work experience.' If a job is asking for '3+ years of experience working with digital signal processing algorithms,' for instance, does a doctorate in which you worked consistently with such algorithms count? My answer is usually yes... *if* you can demonstrate that you can *apply your skills and expertise from this research to the employer's goals and problems.* The question as to whether employers will further value postdoctoral experience has a similar answer: yes, if you can use it to demonstrate how your extra technical skills, leadership competence, ability to manage others, and so on, *will help you do what the employer needs you to do.* The exercises in the 'get to work' section below are designed to help you with this, and to avoid the dreaded accusation of being 'overqualified.'

Get to work

Exercise 6.1: Showing you can help the employer achieve their goals

Before starting an application, the following exercise can help you to align what you say about yourself with the employer's needs, and to focus your application on your most relevant evidence. Step one involves carefully considering the job description and requirements for the role. To demonstrate how this works, let's use the example in Box 6.1.

Box 6.1 Example job advert

Assistant Editor: Educational Publishing

The Assistant Editor provides administrative and editorial support to editors and fosters strong working relationships with authors of textbooks and other educational resources. Responsibilities of the job include:

- Competitor and market research
- Management of peer review process for manuscript drafts
- Analysis of reviews and manuscript drafts
- Planning and preparation of material for websites that accompany textbooks
- Communicating with other departments and with academic authors

Role requirements

- Excellent communication skills.
- Strong attention to detail.
- Experience of the peer review process.
- A strong academic background and an awareness of the resource needs of students in Higher Education.
- Market research skills.
- The ability to work in a fast-paced environment and work to tight deadlines.

Rather than looking for someone who is skilled in communication, attention to detail, and research *in general*, this publishing company is looking for someone who can apply these skills to this specific role. The next step is to connect the requirements for the role with how they directly apply to the activities in the job description. This allows you to compose a profile of the type of person that the employer is seeking. To do this, devise a list of the employer's needs for the role by starting each item with the words 'someone who can.' It helps if each item in your list references one skill from the requirements and one activity in the job description. For example, for the assistant editor role, the company wants:

- **Someone who can** communicate professionally and diplomatically with academic authors.
- **Someone who can** research what other publishers ('competitors') are producing and what students need (i.e. 'market research').
- **Someone who can** review academic writing accurately and at a quick pace.
- **Someone who can** get responses from peer reviewers within tight deadlines.

Now you have your 'someone who can' profile for the role, you can select the best examples from your experience that show you can do these things. Let's take bullet points in a CV for instance, using 'communication skills' as an example. Now, if we simply worked through the role requirements and showed examples of each one, then for communication skills we might come up with something like this:

- Produced an original 80,000-word PhD thesis, demonstrating excellent communication skills.

However, this example focuses on communication through academic writing, which isn't the type of communication undertaken by an assistant editor. As the 'someone who can' profile for the role shows, what is actually needed is someone who can communicate appropriately with academic authors and build good relationships with them. Consequently, a more relevant bullet point would be:

- Compiled proceedings for a national literature conference by managing timely email communication with 12 academic authors to meet a tight two-month deadline.

This doesn't just show communication skills; it demonstrates the kind of communication skills that this employer needs to achieve their goals. However, it does come from someone with specific previous experience of editorial work. Even without such 'direct' experience though, it is still possible to show relevant skills through the broader experience you *do* have, for example:

- Communicated effectively with senior academic supervisors from different disciplines to align expectations and agree on a shared, actionable research brief that enabled the project to proceed.

This example also shows why leaving your doctorate or postdoc off your CV is unwise. Not only would this create a gap in your experience; it might also 'hide' useful experience that shows the employer you can do what they need you to do. Rather than omitting your academic experience, the 'someone who can' method instead helps you to translate it effectively, using it to show how you can help the employer to achieve their goals.

Working out an employer's problems or goals can be difficult from the job advert alone. This is why hearing from people who work for similar employers or have similar roles can help you to do this much more reliably. This is also a way to develop your commercial awareness: that is, your awareness of how your sector(s) of interest operate(s), what they value, and what challenges they face.

To help you with this:

- Identify and attend any relevant events where alumni or guests now working in different fields talk about their experiences.
- Use online communities such as 'Alt Ac Careers' or 'The Professor Is Out' (both on Facebook) to see if you can find and chat to people who have moved into relevant sectors or roles.
- Use the LinkedIn 'alumni search' tricks from Chapter 3 to connect with alumni working in organisations or roles that you are targeting. If they accept, a message like this could help you to find out more from them:

Dear X,
Thank you for connecting, and hello from <the university/ place that you have in common>. I am currently doing a doctorate/postdoc at XXXX and can see that you also did XXXX here with XXXX. I'm interested in working in XXXX and finding out more about what the role of XXXX really entails. I therefore wondered whether you might be willing to share any details about the focus of your role, or any aspects of it that may not have been obvious from the job advert? Any tips by message would be great, or if you had time for a quick call in the next two weeks then that would be fantastic.

Many thanks,
X

If you are really struggling to translate your experience, you could also call on an AI large language model to help. Many organisations now use Applicant Tracking Systems (ATS): software that scans application documents for keywords before they are reviewed by human recruiters. If your application doesn't contain those key words then it may end up in the 'no' pile, even if you're qualified for the role. With specific, targeted prompts, you can use an AI tool to help you choose your most convincing examples and express them in a way that means they won't fly under the ATS radar. For example:

- 'I have several examples of communication experience listed below. Based on this job description, which one best demonstrates that I have what is needed for this role, and why?'
- 'Rewrite this CV bullet point to emphasise planning, prioritisation, and delivery, using language appropriate for this role in a natural way.'

The key is to use generative AI to support your recalibration, not to produce generic, template-like responses. Recent research highlights employers' growing frustration with monotonous AI-generated applications, with some even noticing the same phrases and answers repeated by multiple candidates (McMahon-Harvey and Morris, 2025). If you do use AI, always review the wording to make sure it still reflects your individual experience and couldn't just be copied and pasted into someone else's application.

Exercise 6.2: Showing your motivation (for dodging 'overqualification')

Being dismissed by employers as 'overqualified' is another common concern amongst doctoral and postdoctoral researchers: but what does this really mean? Rather than implying that you're too good for the job, labelling you as overqualified often has more to do with an employer's worries that you won't be interested or challenged by a role, or that you might get bored and move on quickly, leaving them having to re-recruit. If it's a role you really want, however, or one that you are using to get your foot in the door, a way to quell concerns around overqualification is to carefully outline your *motivation* for applying for the role. Explaining why you want that specific job, and how it links with your previous experience and future goals, can help convince employers that their opportunity is a conscious career choice for you, not just a 'stop gap' or a panic application.

The ease (or difficulty) that you experience in explaining your motivation for a job can also be revealing. Unless you have particular challenges around writing and storytelling in general, chances are that if trying to explain your motivation for a role drains your energy, it probably isn't the role for you. Instead, switching your focus to roles where your motivation story comes more naturally could help you find a better fit.

A paragraph near the beginning of your cover letter or supporting statement is a good place to state your motivation. Make the paragraph specific and personal, and not something that you could copy and paste into applications for other jobs. For example, here is what you want to avoid:

> I am keen to continue my career in your esteemed company; your commitment to innovation and being at the cutting edge of clean energy closely align with my own values. I am now looking to apply my research and technical skills to a role with real world impact and would relish the opportunity to do this as a member of your team.

This example is too general, doesn't give any evidence for its claims, and doesn't demonstrate an understanding of the role or the hiring company. Compare it with this more specific example:

> I have a long-standing interest in clean energy, as demonstrated by my attendance at events including the Renewable Fuels Expo. This Energy Systems Modeller role particularly appeals to me as these events have shown me how big data and modelling can facilitate far more effective decision making to improve energy systems. I am therefore particularly keen to apply my data analysis, stochastic modelling, and problem-solving skills to a role like this, to help further establish Organisation X as a leading consultancy in the global transition to clean energy. I would particularly look forward to using your in-house energy modelling suite to further develop my modelling skills whilst making a real difference for clients.

This motivation paragraph has three key parts:

1. Expression of interest in the broad focus of the job, supported by some evidence (the candidate's attendance at relevant events).
2. Expression of interest in this specific role, including how it contributes to the organisation's wider goals.
3. Expression of what the role 'adds' for the candidate (i.e. how it would help them to develop and therefore not be bored), with specific reference to something that the organisation offers.

Take an example job you wish to apply for and practise composing your motivation paragraph by using these three parts. This will also be very useful in live or recorded interviews, if you are asked questions around what attracted you to apply for that role.

I have a proven interest in ________________________, *as demonstrated by* __________________________________

____

____

____

This particular role appeals to me because ____________

____

____

____

I would particularly look forward to ____________________

____

____

For some employers, 'overqualification' may also involve the perception that candidates moving from academia expect higher salaries. Consequently, make sure that any salary expectations you are asked to indicate are supported by evidence. For example, explaining that your stated salary is based on an average offered for similar roles in the same location (which you could work out from other job adverts, or by using websites like Check-a-Salary, or the 'salaries' section of Glassdoor) can help to show reasonable expectations. If negotiating a higher salary, then offering tangible evidence of how you closely meet (or even exceed) some of the role requirements *beyond just the level of academic qualification stated* will help to show that you don't expect special treatment purely because you have a doctorate or postdoc on your CV.

Exercise 6.3: Identifying 'friendly employers' (for avoiding stereotypes)

Another way of potentially avoiding negative stereotypes in the recruitment process is to target employers who have a track record of hiring people out of academia, as some of the studies highlighted above suggest. Finding out where previous doctoral and postdoctoral researchers have gone on to work can help with this, as can using LinkedIn to identify whether organisations you might be interested in have hired doctorate holders in the past (and if so, into what roles). Not only could this help you to find potential employers who will value your academic experience and credentials; it could also help you to identify companies and organisations where you might be surrounded by like-minded colleagues with shared experiences.

To identify employers who are most likely to be positive about hiring doctorate holders, try out these LinkedIn tricks.

If you are interested in working for a particular organisation(s):

- Type the organisation name into LinkedIn and go to their LinkedIn page.
- On the menu across the middle, click 'people.'
- Click into the search bar within in the 'people' section and type 'PhD' (or your doctoral abbreviation, e.g. EngD, etc.) then hit enter.
- This will show you profiles of employees who have (or are pursuing) a doctorate. Looking through their profiles lets you see the roles they have now, as well as the level of role at which they started. This could help you to figure out the typical 'entry level(s)' for someone moving into that organisation from academia.
- If you then meet a representative from this organisation at a conference or a careers fair and they are unsure whether their company hires people moving from academia, you can use your research to highlight some examples and to ask for a contact from the most relevant team or department.

If you don't have a specific organisation in mind:

- Go to your university's LinkedIn page.
- On the menu across the middle, select 'alumni.'

- Use the filters to find a useful sample of alumni, for example, from 'where they live' choose your preferred location, or from 'what they are skilled at' type in a specific skill that you have.
- Click into the search bar within in the 'alumni' section and type 'PhD' (or your doctoral abbreviation) then hit enter.
- The profiles in your search results will show you where these people work, giving you examples of organisations who have previously employed doctorate holders.

Case study

Now we've covered the basics of how to articulate your skills and experience effectively to employers, this section uses examples to help you apply these principles to your own situation. The featured examples are from a humanities researcher, but the wider techniques shown by these examples are applicable across disciplines and industries.

Case study 6.1: CV evolution

This case study presents three different versions of the first section of a candidate's CV for the Assistant Editor position outlined in Box 6.1. Consider the example CV sections in Boxes 6.2– 6.4 alongside the job advert, and complete the following questions:

1. Imagine you are the employer. What first impression does each version make?

2 How well does each version show that the candidate can do what the employer needs them to do?
3 In what ways does each version risk supporting, or help to challenge, employers' potential stereotypes about researchers?

Box 6.2 CV section example 1

Research experience

PhD English Literature

University of Sometown **2021–2025**

Thesis title: The Narrative Agency of Abandoned Spaces in the Contemporary British Novel

My research thesis takes Lefebvre's theory of the social production of space and applies it to an exploration of the changing role of abandoned buildings in the contemporary British Novel (1979–present). Background information on the ways in which abandoned spaces represent social and political upheaval is provided, and such representations are analysed in a range of popular and independent-press novels. The thesis for the first time combines affect theory with spatial theory to demonstrate how and why abandoned spaces in contemporary novels acquire an agency of their own, over and above that of human actors.

Box 6.3 CV section example 2

Relevant experience

Doctoral Researcher in English Literature

University of Sometown **2021–2025**

- Produced a thesis and article for peer-reviewed academic journal
- Involved in committee for student-led departmental conference (2022–2024)
- Co-edited a volume of essays
- Taught seminars for undergraduates across a range of modules

Box 6.4 CV section example 3

Relevant experience

Doctoral Researcher in English Literature

University of Sometown **2021–2025**

- Developed sound understanding of peer review process, reviewing abstracts for two academic conferences and responding to reviewers' comments on my own work
- Compiled proceedings for a national literature conference by managing timely email

communication with 12 academic authors to meet a tight two-month deadline
- Led seminars for undergraduates and created resource guides across two modules, gaining direct experience in identifying and addressing the learning needs of higher education students.

Case study 6.1 Responses

CV section example 1 (Box 6.2):

- Gives too much technical detail about the candidate's research which isn't immediately relevant to the role. Doing this means you risk coming across as 'too academic,' and as lacking awareness of what is involved in the job(s) for which you have applied.
- Is entitled 'Research Experience,' when this isn't a research-focused role. Doing this could suggest that research or academia are still your priorities, rather than the sector to which you have applied.
- Gives a dense paragraph of text which is difficult to read at speed. In a study using eye-tracking technology, US-based job search firm Ladders (2018) found that the average first screen of a CV by a recruiter was just 7.4 seconds, so whatever your academic background or target sector, your CV needs to be quickly scannable.

CV section example 2 (Box 6.3):

- Is entitled 'Relevant Experience,' suggesting transferability and openness to moving to another sector.
- Uses bullet points, which are easier to scan at speed than dense paragraphs.
- Focuses bullet points on experiences more relevant to the role. BUT…
- Describes 'things the person did' rather than clear examples that prove that they can do what the employer needs them to do.

CV section example 3 (Box 6.4):

- Is still easier to read quickly.
- Uses bullet points, each of which gives a clear example of something the employer needs. Doing this makes it easy for the employer to see how your experience is relevant, without having to spend time working this out themselves.
- Shows the impact of the person's work, using numbers and scale. This technique can help employers to 'visualise' the difference you made, and to see how you can apply your skills in real-world situations.

Boxes 6.5 and 6.6 contain further tips from two real recruiters on how to maximise the impact of your CV for sectors beyond academia.

Box 6.5 Recruiter's perspective

Kate

Early Career Recruiter

Obtaining a doctorate is an incredible achievement which will have equipped you with lots of skills that are transferrable into the workplace. Occasionally though, I see applications from researchers where these broader skills and knowledge aren't explicit within the application itself. It may be that the individual has focused heavily on the subject area of their research and hasn't necessarily sold the other skills that they've obtained, whether that's project management, communication, analytical skills and everything else in between. The ability to personalise a job application to let your motivations and interests shine through can be really difficult, especially if you're used to writing professional academic reports. It's that personal touch, however, that can make the impact when recruiters are screening multiple applications.

Box 6.6 Recruiter's perspective

Sarah

Former Recruiter

Your CV is usually the first opportunity for you to show recruiters and employers your potential. Be concise and try to limit your CV to a maximum of two to three pages. Include key words and phrases such as 'managed,' 'developed,' 'improved' and 'achieved' to illustrate where you have made a difference, instead of merely listing what you have done. Key skills that recruiters and employers will be looking for include analytical, communication, organisational skills, and time management. Evidence of giving presentations or leading seminars and conferences during your time in academia will demonstrate your communication skills. Perhaps you've led a project or managed an event where you've had deadlines to meet and had to organise not just your own but other people's time – all relevant experience.

Soft skills are also crucial to employers, as transitioning into industry will involve dealing with cross-functional departments, so employers will be looking for someone who is going to be a good team fit. Any examples of where you have worked as part of a team will show your ability to collaborate, communicate, and respond to different situations and challenges. This could be as part of your research, a job outside of your doctorate, or even any volunteering you may have done.

Case study 6.2 Letter or statement evolution

Above, we outlined good technique for addressing your motivation in a cover letter or supporting statement. This next case study presents two versions of a section of a cover letter addressing why someone is a good candidate for the role, again referring to the Assistant Editor position. Consider each version in boxes 6.7 and 6.8, and complete the following questions:

1 Imagine you are the employer. What first impression does each version make?
2 How well does each version show that the candidate can do what the employer needs them to do?
3 In what ways does each version risk supporting, or help to challenge, employers' potential stereotypes about researchers?

Box 6.7 Cover letter section example 1

I have a range of experience that I could bring to the Assistant Editor role. During my PhD, I wrote an original 80,000-word thesis and article for peer-reviewed academic journal and also co-edited a volume of essays. Throughout my PhD I regularly communicated with a range of academics from PhD students to senior professors. I have also led lectures and seminars for undergraduate students. I would enjoy bringing these experiences to the role of Assistant Editor.

Box 6.8 Cover letter section example 2

I am experienced in communicating tactfully and diplomatically with academics, which would be valuable in this role. For example, during my PhD I had two senior academic supervisors who disagreed on the scope of my project, which threatened to delay the submission date. To address this, I proposed a solution that combined one supervisor's theoretical approach with the other's demand for practical case studies. They both agreed with my proposal, and my management of the situation established a productive working relationship that led to me completing the project on time. This shows that I have the communication skills required to build good relationships with academics, and would feel confident in liaising with academic authors on potentially sensitive matters such as peer review feedback and editorial deadlines in the role of Assistant Editor.

Case study 6.2 Responses

Cover letter section example 1 (box 6.7):

- Simply repeats details already on the person's CV in prose form.
- Lists things that the person has done rather than giving specific examples.
- Does not say how these experiences will help the candidate to do the job well, and help the

employer achieve their goals. Doing this may lead the employer to presume that you don't understand what is involved in the role.

Cover letter section example 2 (box 6.8):

- Focuses on a specific example, showing the scale and impact of the person's work.
- Summarises key abilities shown by this example, which are relevant to the role.
- Explicitly shows which aspect of the job this experience would help the candidate to perform well. Doing this helps the employer to see exactly how your experience is relevant and shows 'what's in for them' if they hire you!

Case study 6.3 Interview answers

All the tips we have covered are also applicable to interview preparation. Researching the role and the company will be useful for questions about your motivation for applying, as well as commercial awareness questions around what the organisation does, who its competitors are, and the challenges it may face in current social, economic, and political circumstances. Preparing examples of when you have previously demonstrated skills required for the role, or have done things similar to the activities involved in the role, will help you to support your claims with evidence.

To end this chapter, let's look at an example answer to the interview question:

'Tell me about a time when you failed to meet a deadline and what you learned from this.'

> Last year, I had a deadline to submit a progress report for my section of a research project in the same week as the deadline for a blog article I'd been invited to write by a charity where I volunteer. As it was the first time I'd done a progress report, I underestimated how much time it would take. When I realised that I was running behind with the report, I contacted the project leader to apologise and to take accountability for my error in planning. I negotiated a revised deadline for the report and made this revised deadline a top priority, writing out a report plan and using my Outlook calendar to apportion time to each part. In the end, my blog article was published on time, my progress report was approved, and the project leader also then trusted me with the responsibility of mentoring a junior member of the team as well. This experience showed me how important it is to be accountable for my own errors; nobody is perfect, but being transparent helped me maintain a good relationship with my senior colleague in this case. As an Assistant Editor, I would take time early in the role to get a clear picture of how long key processes take so that

I can manage multiple deadlines for peer reviews, manuscript reviews, and other tasks effectively.

This example answer:

- Gives a clear and specific situation.
- Outlines what the candidate did in the situation, and the result of this. Doing this helps the employer clearly visualise how you deal with situations and how you manage yourself at work.
- Shows what the candidate learned from this situation (especially important in questions that focus on weaknesses or times when things haven't gone to plan).
- Says how the example given shows they would be able to do what the employer needs them to do. Doing this makes it really clear to the employer how your experience is applicable.

Takeaways

- Research shows that doctoral and postdoctoral researchers often find it challenging to translate their experience in ways that resonate with employers beyond academia, and which demonstrate their ability to operate in more commercial environments.
- Studies also show that some employers hold stereotypes about candidates coming from doctoral or postdoctoral research. These include being too

narrowly specialised, finding it difficult to adapt to non-academic working environments and work to tight timescales and budgets, and lacking interest in work beyond academia.

- There is often a disconnect between the skills that academics think are most important, and those that are most valued by employers beyond academia. During the recruitment process, this can reinforce employers' stereotypes about researchers.
- Identifying an employer's needs, reflecting on how you present yourself, and bringing these two things into alignment, is therefore crucial to creating convincing applications and preparing for interviews.
- A way to achieve such alignment and mitigate negative stereotypes is to show how you can help the employer to achieve their goals or to solve their key problems.
- Clearly articulating your motivation for a particular role can also help you to create convincing applications and to assuage employers' reservations that you may be 'overqualified.'
- Evidence shows that employers with experience of hiring doctorate holders are more likely to rate their skills positively. Another way to avoid negative stereotypes, therefore, is to target employers with a track record of hiring people with higher degrees and former academics.

References

Boyd, R. and McAlinden, S. (2016) *PhD Study to Employment: Experiences of Transition*. Available at: https://luminate.prospects.ac.uk/phd-study-to-employment-experiences-of-transition [Accessed 9 December 2024].

Caterine, C. (2020) *Leaving Academia: A Practical Guide*. Princeton, NJ: Princeton University Press.

Chen, L., Mewburn, I., Suominen, H. and Grant, W. (2026) 'PhD employability beyond academia: an analysis of industry skills emphasis through a cultural capital lens,' *Higher Education Research & Development*, pp. 1–19. doi: 10.1080/07294360.2025.2515212.

Council for Industry and Higher Education (2010) *Talent Fishing: What Businesses Want from Postgraduates*. London: CIHE. Available at: https://www.ncub.co.uk/reports/talent-fishing-what-businesses-want-from-postgraduates.html [Accessed 9 December 2024].

Diamond, A., Ball, C., Vorley, T., Hughes, T., Moreton, R., Howe, P. and Nathwani, T. (2014) *The Impact of Doctoral Careers* [online]. Leicester: CFE Research. Available at: https://www.ncub.co.uk/insight/the-impact-of-doctoral-careers/ [Accessed 20 October 2024].

Garcia-Quevedo, J., Mas-Verdú, F. and Polo-Otero, J. (2012) 'Which firms want PhDs? An analysis of the determinants of the demand,' *Higher Education*, 63, pp. 607–620. doi: 10.1007/s10734-011-9461-8.

Hayter, C. and Parker, M. (2019) 'Factors that influence the transition of university postdocs to non-academic scientific careers: an exploratory study,' *Research Policy*, 48(3), pp. 556–570. doi: 10.1016/j.respol.2018.09.009.

Hankel, I. (2023). *The Power of a PhD: How Anyone Can Use Their PhD to Get Hired in Industry.* New York: Morgan James.

Ladders (2018) *Eye-Tracking Study.* Available at: https://www.theladders.com/static/images/basicSite/pdfs/TheLadders-EyeTracking-StudyC2.pdf [Accessed 16 June 2025].

McMahon-Harvey, C. and Morris, K. (2025) *Applying for jobs and generative AI: What do employers really think?* Graduate Market Trends. Available at: https://luminate.prospects.ac.uk/what-employers-really-think-about-ai-in-job-applications [Accessed 29 December 2025].

Muurlink, O., Chen, L., Boorman, R., Pearson, D. and Cohen, G. (2024) 'Stakeholder perceptions of what industry wants from doctoral students: a systematic literature review,' *Higher Education Research & Development*, 43(4), pp. 952–965. doi: 10.1080/07294360.2023.2269871.

Peacey, S. and Romijn, L. (2026) *What Do Postdocs Do Next?* [online]. Cambridge: University of Cambridge Careers Service. Available at: https://www.careers.cam.ac.uk/careers-support-postdocs/what-do-postdocs-do-next [Accessed 21 January 2026].

Persson, T. (ed.) (2025). *Job Hunting for the 21st Century: A Comprehensive Guide for the Modern PhD.* Cambridge: Royal Society of Chemistry.

Rubio, M. and Hooley, T. (2010) *Recruiting Researchers: Survey of Employer Practice 2009* [online]. Cambridge: The Careers Research and Advisory Centre. Available at: https://derby-repository.worktribe.com/output/804914/recruiting-researchers-survey-of-employer-practice-2009 [Accessed 1 October 2024].

Suomi, K., Kuoppakangas, P., Kivistö, J., Stenvall, J. and Pekkola, E. (2020) 'Exploring doctorate holders' perceptions of the non-academic labour market and reputational problems they relate to their employment,' *Tertiary Education and Management,* 26, pp. 397–414. doi: 10.1007/s11233-020-09061-1.

Tardelli, M. (2023) *Beyond Academia: Stories and Strategies for PhDs Making the Leap to Industry.* Self-published.

7 Your new start beyond academia

Just as romantic comedies usually end with the wedding, a lot of advice on careers beyond academia ends at the job offer. But what if it isn't all happily ever after? Ultimately, career transition is a process, and adjusting to your new employer(s), role(s), and colleagues may take time and patience. In this final chapter, therefore, we look at some of the potential challenges involved in managing this adjustment period and what you can do to mitigate them.

Ultimately, it is unlikely that your first job beyond academia will be perfect, whatever that means for you. However, it will likely give you a vantage point from which to survey your new sector, and life beyond academia, more broadly. Once you start your new role(s), you may be exposed to teams, departments, and opportunities that you didn't previously know existed, giving you information about your future options and preferences that is only available from 'the inside.' This chapter is designed to help you apply what you've learned from this book to navigating your new role(s) with confidence and purpose. To begin, we'll look at what evidence has to say about common challenges involved in adapting to life beyond academia, and what to look out for as you take your next steps.

DOI: 10.4324/9781003589785-8

What's the evidence?

Studies paint a mixed picture of how easily researchers adjust to careers beyond academia. Some suggest that, even though moving into other sectors often involves different expectations, a faster pace of work, and less autonomy over workloads, many researchers adapt with relatively few difficulties (e.g. De Grande et al., 2014: 546). Others, however, portray the transition as involving a more pronounced sense of 'culture shock.'

Amongst former postdocs, for example, Hayter and Parker (2019) identified more rigid working schedules beyond academia, and the need to switch from individual research objectives to working in a team towards shared goals, as factors that can make the transition particularly challenging (562). Meanwhile, other triggers may include the switch to more formal structures of line management, conflict between tight deadlines and perfectionism, lack of recognition for one's expertise, and the need to adapt to new working methods such as more concise writing styles, the latter meaning that some researchers report experiencing 'a destabilising period during which they had to completely relearn certain tasks' in order to adjust to their new professional environments (Skakni et al., 2022:1279). Transferring skills from academia to other sectors can therefore take some work, requiring you to 'add new dimensions' to your skill set to make it work in your new context (Chen et al., 2026: 12). Having spent years developing expertise and recognition in a particular research field, to then have to relearn how you approach fundamental work activities like writing and presenting could well impact your confidence and evoke feelings of imposterism. This was something I certainly experienced in my own professional transition; during my doctoral research I'd started to feel established in a particular field, but for my first year as a careers adviser I felt unsettled, like I was floundering to get to grips with my new profession and wondering if this had all been a terrible mistake.

As well as the impact of practical differences, taking your career beyond academia may also require adjustment to new social and sensory norms, including adapting how you interact with others and showing tact and diplomacy within your new workplace(s) (Skakni et al., 2022: 1278). Changing sectors may also require a shift from maintaining close ties with others in your field to managing relationships with a far wider network of teams and stakeholders (Li and Horta, 2024: 427). This can also bring changes to your sensory environment, such as having to switch from working independently in academia to 'being in an office of like fifty people, with people like constantly talking around you' (Boyd and McAlinden, 2016: 20). Being used to quieter academic working environments may make the shared office spaces and increased collaboration of some other sectors overwhelming, especially if you are neurodivergent or experience other challenges around social interaction and sensory overstimulation.

Moving beyond academia isn't just a shift in working practices and environments, it's also a shift in *community*. During your doctoral or postdoctoral research, you may have been part of an academic community comprising other researchers in your lab, department, or discipline with whom you have shared experiences and interests. As Anne Krook describes in her blog for doctoral and postdoctoral researchers, joining a new community of colleagues with whom you may not yet have so much in common can provoke feelings of loneliness (Krook, no date), which might be intensified if you also miss aspects of your former academic work such as supervising students, teaching, or contributing to scholarship in an area for which you still have a passion. However, Krook argues that whilst many former academics tend to focus on the *differences* between academia and their new workplaces, those who tend to be happiest and adapt more quickly are those who also focus on the *similarities*, 'of learning new things, of researching, of solving problems, of expressing the solutions clearly in writing and speaking' (Krook, no date).

As well as adapting to changes in working practices, environments, and communities, transitioning into your new role(s) may also involve navigating your feelings about the work itself. For example, whilst some studies find no evidence of lower job satisfaction amongst doctorate holders employed beyond academia than those within the academy (e.g. Lawson & Lopes-Bento, 2024), others suggest that doctoral graduates are significantly less likely to be highly satisfied with their jobs if they feel their skills are being underused (e.g. Paolo and Mañé, 2016). Consequently, just as disillusionment with academia may catalyse many researchers' career changes into other sectors, so is it important to acknowledge the possibility of experiencing disillusionment on leaving academia too, especially if your first role leaves you feeling underemployed.

Finally, challenges may also emerge in juggling your new role with any continuing academic responsibilities. Some participants in Boyd and McAlinden's study referenced above reported having to find work before finishing their doctorates, making it tricky to find time to fit academic work around attending interviews and starting their new jobs (2016: 21). It goes without saying that getting to grips with a new role and new working environment during the day, then coming home to write up research in the evening has the potential to leave anyone feeling stretched, stressed, and tired. On the other hand, you may actively want to stay involved in academia alongside your new role, for example by maintaining links with your academic discipline or by continuing to teach. Whether it's finishing up or staying involved, this introduces questions as to how to make your new role work alongside other commitments, and how you might be able to negotiate this with your new employer.

What does this mean for you?

It's no wonder that transitioning into work beyond academia might leave you facing some existential questions. When adjusting to a new working environment, getting to grips with different ways of working, and adapting to new social situations – all whilst you may still be wrapping up previous academic work – it's common to experience feelings of being 'in-between' identities. It's normal that moving away from academia can feel destabilising, and re-establishing a clear sense of who you are professionally may well take time and patience.

Whilst liminality may feel like your new reality, now that you have put the career change cogs in motion you can start to carve out your new professional identity. One way to do this is to revisit the question from Chapter 2 about which aspects of your current work you would like to keep and which you would like to change. Once you start your new role(s) beyond academia, asking yourself this at regular intervals is a useful way to:

- Appreciate what you are enjoying about your new role(s) and working environment(s).
- Acknowledge what you are finding difficult, and how this can be addressed.
- Consider the extent to which you are using skills that you most want to use in your work.
- Recognise anything you may miss about life in academia, and what you might be able to do about this.
- Take stock of how you feel about who you are now, in a professional sense.

In whatever ways your new professional life may feel defamiliarising, liminal, and imperfect, there are plenty of things you can try to make it feel a bit more like *yours.*

Job crafting

Underuse of your skills, misalignment with your values, or missing aspects of your former academic work aren't necessarily things you just have to accept, or indicators of the need for another complete career change. In their popular *Squiggly Careers* framework, for example, Tupper and Ellis advocate for 'job crafting': the process of shaping your current role to better align with your strengths and values (2020: 42). In our terms, job crafting refers to ways in which you can use your current role to bring your work more in line with your keep/lose/add profile from Chapter 2. Anne Krook specifically applies the concept of job crafting to post-academic careers, noting how many activities that former academics tend to miss about academia can be found in other guises elsewhere: for example, mentoring junior colleagues has much in common with supervising students, whilst training interns or making presentations are akin to teaching (no date).

You may also want to add things to your new role that you don't currently get the chance to do. Or perhaps there are actions that you can take to try out new professional identities within your current role, to help build up a sense of your new working self. You may even find that you miss aspects of your previous academic work. If any of these situations transpire for you, then some job crafting actions to consider include:

- Getting involved in projects that allow you use certain skills, or gain exposure to a different type of team, client, responsibility, etc.
- Consider what you might like to be known for in your new workplace or sector – whether that is specific knowledge or expertise, strengths, or something else – and seek out opportunities to take steps towards this.
- Thinking *why* you miss a certain aspect of your previous work or *why* you want to add something specific into your current role, and considering what activities happen in your current workplace that might allow you to exercise similar skills or achieve a similar fulfilment. This could include things such as involvement in staff training or university outreach, or taking part in staff groups or networks that allow you to stay connected to a particular interest.
- If you miss being part of a scholarly community, scope out possibilities to negotiate with your employer for time to undertake external activities like teaching. In addition, explore what the equivalent of a scholarly community is in your new line of work: for example,

whether there are conferences that your colleagues attend, or associations or societies in which they take part.
- Raising your suggestions with a line manager in a 1:1 meeting or review.

Exploring options from the inside

Beginning your new role beyond academia offers you an inside view of your new company or organisation, and also your new sector. For example, you might be flourishing in your new role and therefore wondering what options this could open up for you longer term. On the other hand, you might feel like the role you've moved into isn't the best use of your skills and strengths and have a nagging feeling that something's missing. In either case, there are ways you can use your new role and corresponding networks to explore alternative or future options. These include:

- Gauging your relationship with your line manager or equivalent(s): could you talk to them about your interests in finding out what colleagues in other areas of the organisation do? See Cat's story in case study 7.2 for an example of this.
- Taking formal opportunities to find out about the work of different teams and colleagues, for example through staff networks or events.
- Informal networking with colleagues to find out about their roles and experiences. Take opportunities to find out about what other teams do (e.g. through internal communications, following up after meetings, asking your manager for introductions, etc.).

Adapting to new ways of working

Chances are that your doctoral or postdoctoral research has already given you a wealth of experience in getting up to speed and teaching yourself new things. If, however, adjusting to your new workplace is proving a steep learning curve, it's unlikely that you'll be expected to navigate this alone. Some actions you can take to get up to speed include:

- Reflecting on instances where you had to learn new things or adapt to new ways of working in your research, and how you can apply these to your current situation.
- Is there a professional body or association that represents people who work in your new sector? If so, can your employer grant you membership? These types of organisations may offer networking opportunities or training aimed at people new to the profession.
- Looking at examples of work similar to what you will need to deliver, to familiarise yourself with expectations around writing style, how reports are structured, and so on.
- Finding clarity on what you're expected to achieve in a new job can be challenging initially, especially if the role has been newly created. Talking to your manager(s) about what success would look like and agreeing on some initial objectives can help you to establish some direction and purpose.

Coping with imposterism

Academic culture can sometimes make us feel that we can only 'earn the right' to work in a particular area if we're a recognised expert in it. Whilst this can lead to feeling like an imposter when first moving into another sector, it's important to acknowledge that you, like everyone, are a work in progress. To manage any feelings of imposterism or crises of confidence in your new role:

- Accept that not knowing everything is ok, and check if you are holding yourself to higher standards than your colleagues.
- Keep lines of communication open with your manager(s), especially around your training needs and things you are finding difficult.
- Don't give yourself a hard time for making a few mistakes. In a year's time, will those mistakes still matter? Will anyone really remember them? If not, reflect, extract the learning, and move on.
- Practice patience. In their study of doctoral graduates in the UK, Bryan and Guccione (2018) found that the value that participants attached to their doctorate increased over time from the point of graduation (1132). This was attributed to the ways in which increased time since graduation allowed for greater reflection on the usefulness of one's doctorate for current employment, and the relevance of skills and status derived from the doctorate becoming more apparent over time. What this study does not acknowledge, is that this result could also be influenced by the fact that spending more time in their new roles may have led participants to develop greater feelings of competence in these roles. In turn, this may result in greater enjoyment of the role and more positive portrayals of how their doctorate had helped them into a meaningful career. Even if you initially struggle to see how your research experience qualifies you for your new role, evidence

suggests that as you grow in competence and confidence, the more likely you are to feel that your doctorate or postdoc was 'worth it.'

Adjusting to different physical and social conditions

Adapting to the different physical, sensory, and social conditions of your new workplace(s) can be challenging, especially if you have a disability or health condition. To help advocate for your needs:

- Be open with your line manager(s) about how your new work environment differs from what you have been used to previously. This will help to prevent them making assumptions about what you are, and aren't, familiar with.
- If you have a disability, health condition, or other circumstances that impact your interaction with your working environment, find out what support is available. Make note of your triggers and how your condition affects you at work, inform your manager(s) of any workplace adjustments that you need, and ask about your employer's budget to cover these.
- Ask for details of any arrangements your new employer might offer for hybrid or flexible working, if a combination of on-site and remote working would benefit you.
- Enquire whether your workplace offers mentoring or a 'buddy' scheme to help orientate new members of staff.
- Research what other internal resources may be helpful. This may include resources like a company intranet

that explains standard practices and processes, or even staff networks linked to protected characteristics or personal circumstances, such as a women's network or a disabled staff network. If you don't learn about these initiatives in an induction, ask whether they exist.

- Although starting a new job can be hectic, make time for the things that help to keep you balanced, like keeping in touch with friends and former colleagues, physical activity, hobbies, and other interests.

Get to work

In Chapter 2, we looked at how to get started on exploring your next steps by asking yourself three simple questions:

If I were to turn what I'm doing now (be it a PhD, a postdoc, an academic job, etc.) into my ideal job:

- *What aspects of it would I want to* ***keep?***
- *What aspects of it would I want to* ***lose?***
- *What aspects would I want to* **add** *to it that I don't have at the moment?*

However, your 'keep/lose/add' profile isn't just a tool to kick start your career transition: it's a tool that you can use throughout your career to continue 'tweaking' your professional activities according to your preferences and priorities.

As you begin your new role(s) beyond academia, regularly check in with yourself by revisiting your keep/lose/add profile. Whether there are things you miss from your previous academic life, bits of yourself that you don't get to use as much as you'd like to, or parts of your new role or organisation that you would like to explore further, use the keep/lose/add framework to take stock of how things are going, and to plan your next 'tweaks.' You can do this by adding in an extra 'actions' section to each of your items. Table 7.1 shows how to set this out, using my own experiences in my first post-PhD job in student recruitment as an example. Remember, some of the 'aspects' that you might like to keep, lose, or add, include:

- Work activities, i.e. the things that you do every day in your work.
- The environment you are working in, for example, the setting and location of your work.
- The working culture, e.g. supportive, team-based, collaborative, fast-paced, etc.
- How the work fits more personal preferences, including things like flexible working, work-life balance, salary, adjustments for health conditions and disabilities, and so on.

You can use the suggestions in the 'what this means for you' section for inspiration when devising your actions but remember to consider your life outside of work as well. If tweaking your new role in every way you desire isn't feasible, you could consider how you might be able to address some items in your 'add' column through pursuits outside of work.

Case study

This section features four real career stories from contributors who faced challenges with their first roles beyond academia, and used what they learned from these

Table 7.1 Applying the 'Keep lose/add' framework in your new role, using the author's experience as an example

Keep	*Lose*	*Add*
Working environment and team culture: good people and a nice social atmosphere. *Action: when exploring next steps from this role, prioritise getting a sense of the team culture before making a move.*	The 'salesy' aspect of my current role. *Action: identify other roles in my wider department and associated departments that are people-facing and have an advisory aspect, but don't have a sales focus. Find out what would be needed to make a sideways move into these.*	More use of presentation and public speaking skills. *Action: ask manager in next 1:1 meeting about opportunities to deliver talks at events and open days.*

(*Continued*)

Table 7.1 (Continued)

Keep	*Lose*	*Add*
Helping people in their educational and career journeys. *Action: collaborate with colleagues in the careers service to extend my impact in this area.*		More of a network in HE professional services: my network is still mostly focused on my previous academic field. *Action: ask colleagues which professional conferences they attend; ask line manager about staff development budget to scope out which events I can attend this year.* Formal learning – I miss studying (!) *Action: in work, find out what professional qualifications colleagues hold, or are pursuing, and see if any of these fit my interests.* *Also explore learning opportunities outside of work linked to personal interests (for example, I took a course in stand-up comedy…!).*

challenges to 'tweak' their professional activities to better align with their priorities. Read their stories and consider whether you could borrow or adapt any of the actions they took to address issues you are facing in your current role(s), or to help you make the most of your current role.

Case study 7.1 Alice

For the first year after her doctorate, Alice balanced 2.5 days a week in an 'academic adjacent' role in a university with some academic teaching and some consultancy work. 'This was partly intentional and partly out of necessity' Alice explains.

> The time of year I ended up completing and submitting my PhD meant that I was out of step with the cycle for most postdocs, but I also didn't know what kind of career I wanted to pursue. I knew I enjoyed working in higher education, working with students, researching, and 'bridging the gap' between academia and 'industry.' However, I didn't enjoy the hourly paid contracts that can be common in academia.

When the contracts for her academic adjacent role and teaching ended, Alice switched to doing remote freelance consulting work on a full-time basis. 'However,' she describes,

> I soon realised that there were things I missed including working with others,

> having support from an institution, and ultimately, working with students! I found freelancing full-time quite lonely: so much so that after three months I applied for (and was offered) a four-year, part-time research and teaching contract at another university. Part of this new role includes building networks for students to undertake placements in local institutions, continuing the kinds of connections I made during my academic adjacent work.

Alice intends to continue to seek variety in her professional activities, combining student-facing work with other opportunities. She says

> based on the jobs I have had so far, my priorities going forward will be to continue to build up my experience and my networks, and to undertake new opportunities as and when they arise. My freelance consulting work has already allowed me to undertake really interesting roles and to meet new people; for example, I have researched and appeared on a TV documentary and have travelled around the country to meet stakeholders and to provide advice. My four-year academic contract also now offers me some stability in income too, allowing me to continue freelancing around this and to build a career that straddles academia and beyond.

Alice's story shows how much she learned about her preferences from the first 15 months after finishing her doctorate. Some of the key points in her story include:

- Combining different types of work (including fixed-term contracts) post-PhD to try out different things.
- A change in her working situation due to circumstances beyond her control (contracts coming to an end and not being renewed).
- A shift from a 'portfolio' way of working to a full-time remote role.
- Missing specific aspects of working within higher education.
- Reflecting on her more general working preferences (e.g. stable income, having regular contact with others).
- Based on these preferences, pursuing the option to combine a role within higher education with other work beyond the academy, challenging the dichotomy of 'leaving' or 'staying in' academia.

Case study 7.2 Cat

Three and a half years into a permanent academic lectureship position in Biblical Studies, Cat made a career transition into a content writing role for a software company. Her role involved reading pieces of legislation and turning them into accessible summaries. It might sound like quite a leap, but her experience in writing for a range of audiences, editing writing following peer review, and analysing ancient laws were transferable to the role.

However, she soon started to feel frustrated. 'I picked up the work very quickly,' she explains. 'Within a week I was bored: I'd be asked to summarise what was considered to be a very technical law, but would be done by lunchtime!'

Cat felt she underestimated her abilities, saying that

> being able to research and deliver writing was a skill I'd dismissed because in academia you do it without thinking about it. In my new role I was delivering at a faster pace than most because of my experience within academia.

'Yes, I got bored,' says Cat,

> but within a few months I felt confident enough to speak to my manager about other opportunities. They set up conversations for me to have with various people across the company about other potential roles. That's how I found my way into product management, and it's been the biggest and best challenge of my life.

Cat therefore offers reassurance that

> you are very unlikely to move out of academia straight into a role that's perfect. Once you've made the move though, you can then move again; in other sectors it's

> much easier to do this than in academia. Originally, I thought that I couldn't leave academia unless I got a job that I knew that I would love, but then I thought: no, it's ok to go, get your foot in the door, and find a role that buys you the time and the headspace to *then* make the 'right' move and to build a career.

Cat's example shows that even if your first job beyond academia isn't perfect, there are ways you can use it to steer your work into closer alignment with your values and priorities. Key actions that Cat took to do this include:

- Accepting that her first job beyond academia was unlikely to be perfect but was the first step in a process of working out where she might want to be longer term.
- Not accepting boredom and an underuse of her skills as necessities.
- Understanding how her skills 'measured up' in her new working environment and reflecting on what she might be capable of in this new setting.
- Building a positive and open relationship with her line manager which could be leveraged to support her professional development.
- Using her first job beyond academia to meet and talk to people working in a range of different roles in her company, giving her examples of where she might see herself going next.

Case study 7.3 Carlos

After his doctorate in Industrial Engineering, Carlos was working in a research and teaching position at his former university in Spain. Wanting to spend more time focused on research, however, he shifted into a Postdoctoral Research Scientist role at IBM in the UK. Carlos explains that despite industry experience during his undergraduate studies and an internship at a UK university during his PhD, his new role required significant adjustment.

'Even though the role was very closely aligned to my research interests, the differences were significant,' Carlos admits.

> I moved from a relatively small university to one of the largest companies in the world. The time spent on tasks such as internal processes and global alignment was even greater than in academia, which took some getting used to. I also had to learn to balance undertaking research with processes such as project planning, coding best practices, and other industry-related tasks. In terms of adapting to the UK culture compared to Spain, there were also things to learn: language initially posed a barrier, as did certain customs. Nevertheless, I relished the opportunity to work with people from a wide range of disciplines on research that had tangible real-world impact.

In the end, however, Carlos moved back to his hometown in Spain for personal reasons. 'Securing a university position after leaving academia is not easy, and I knew that I also didn't enjoy the teaching load or the lack of agility in academic environments,' he explains.

> So rather than looking for an academic job, I initially considered finding a remote position to work from Spain and sent out CVs to companies. However, I also had ideas and a business plan for founding a startup that aligned with my goals and interests. My partner joined the venture after some time, and we are now working together with technology and solutions related to our research fields. Running my own business at this stage of my career has been a way to combine the applied research and technical work that I enjoyed in industry with a set-up that works for my personal life as well.

Carlos's example shows that even when a role in a sector beyond academia is closely aligned to your research interests and background, differences in how things work between academia and more commercial environments mean that it can take time to adapt. Carlos's story also shows how he built on his industrial experience to then further 'tweak' his career to bring it more in line with his personal circumstances. Key points in Carlos's example include:

- Acknowledging that despite his expertise, he still had a lot to learn in his new working environment.

- The importance of allotting time to learn the processes of your new workplace and the customs of professional etiquette in your new environment or country.
- The fact that 'life happens,' and that with that may come the need to change professional plans due to personal circumstances.
- Remembering why he moved away from academia in the first place and considering wider options so that a change in circumstances did not necessitate 'going back.'
- Working out what would combine the things he enjoyed about industry with the demands of personal circumstances: i.e., using his career experience gathered so far to launch his own venture.

Case study 7.4 Nelly

Following her doctoral research in Modern Greek Studies, Nelly took up a Research Manager role in a consultancy firm that undertakes policy-related research for public sector and third sector clients. She notes that whilst the skills developed in her doctorate were highly transferable, adapting to new ways of working in consultancy presented her with quite a learning curve.

'I found that many of my existing skills were directly transferable: doing literature reviews; primary research (including interviews); and proposal writing were all familiar from my PhD' Nelly explains.

> The biggest difference, however, was the pace: in consulting, I had about one-fifth of

> the time I would have had in academia to complete similar tasks. Another shift was in tone: where academia is cautious and heavily caveats findings, client-oriented research requires you to position yourself as an expert, presenting findings as robust and actionable. Academics tend to undersell their expertise, while in consulting, you need to persuade clients that you are the right researcher for the job.
>
> Another adjustment was working as part of a team because my PhD had been a largely solitary endeavour. I also had to learn new skills, particularly data analysis using Excel and statistical packages, how to manage resources and large budgets, as well as evaluation methodologies that were unfamiliar to me.

Four years on, Nelly is still working in the same field, but has worked for multiple employers since her first job post-PhD. 'My moves have been driven by both personal and professional factors,' she explains,

> seeking things like better work-life balance, greater learning and development opportunities, the right kind of intellectual challenge, and improved pay. Consulting can be intense, so I prioritised an employer that offered flexibility, including remote work and a four-day working week. I've also relocated

to three different cities which played a role in job hopping too. Company culture has also played a big role in my career choices, and these factors will most certainly continue to shape my next steps from here.

Nelly's example shows the possibility of applying your skills to subject matter beyond your previous research experience. In client-facing work like Nelly's, with this may come the need to adapt to new working methods, a change of working pace, and a need to convince clients of the value and credibility of your work.

Key points from Nelly's story include:

- Work beyond academia may involve tasks that feel familiar from your previous experience (e.g. literature reviews, proposal writing, etc.) but may require adapting to a different vocabulary used by your new employer or industry.
- The need to adapt to a faster working pace which does not allow for the same level of depth or detail as academia.
- The need to present yourself as an expert in client-facing work, which could prompt feelings of imposterism if you are used to 'underselling' the value of your work in academia.
- The fact that whilst these adjustments may feel uncomfortable initially, your skills are highly transferable, and it is possible to use these skills to establish yourself as an expert in a field beyond your previous academic expertise.

- Understanding your priorities, and balancing these with your new career area, is a process that can take time.
- Aligning your work with your personal priorities can be as much about factors such as work-life balance, workplace culture, and flexibility, as it is about the type of work or role that you are doing.

Takeaways

- Your first job beyond academia is part of a learning process rather than an 'end goal.'
- Evidence shows that common challenges when moving from academia to other sectors include:
    - Adapting to new ways of working or a different pace of work.
    - Missing aspects of previous academic work.
    - Feeling like an imposter in your new line of work.
    - Adjusting to social and environmental changes in your new workplace.
    - Feeling that your skills and intellect are underused in your new role(s).
    - Balancing starting a new role with finishing up academic work.
- In your new role, use the keep/lose/add framework to identify what's working, what isn't, and what actions will help you feel more confident in your new workplace.
- Getting involved in activities or projects that use the skills you want to use, or that you miss using in academia, can help to better align your work with your priorities.

- Using your current role to explore what other people do within your new organisation or sector can help you to work out where you might see yourself going next.
- Research networks and bodies that can help you to find your feet in your new workplace, such as internal staff networks and 'buddy' schemes, or external organisations like professional societies or associations attached to your new career area.
- Try to establish open communication with your manager(s) from an early stage, to build a foundation for discussing things like workplace adaptations, training needs, and other support you may need.
- Continue to use the keep/lose/add framework throughout your working life to extract learning from your professional experiences, to evaluate how things are going, and to tweak your professional activities according to your changing priorities.

References

Boyd, R. and McAlinden, S. (2016) *PhD Study to Employment: Experiences of Transition*. Available at: https://luminate.prospects.ac.uk/phd-study-to-employment-experiences-of-transition [Accessed 9 December 2024].

Bryan, B. and Guccione, K. (2018) 'Was it worth it? A qualitative exploration into graduate perceptions of doctoral value,' *Higher Education Research & Development*, 37(6), pp. 1124–1140. doi: 10.1080/07294360.2018.1479378.

Chen, L., Mewburn, I., Suominen, H. and Grant, W. (2026) 'PhD employability beyond academia: an analysis of industry skills emphasis through a cultural capital lens,' *Higher Education Research & Development*, pp. 1–19. doi: 10.1080/07294360.2025.2515212.

De Grande, H., De Boyser, K., Vandevelde, K. and Van Rossem, R. (2014) 'From academia to industry: are doctorate holders ready?', *Journal of the Knowledge Economy*, 5(3), pp. 538–561. doi: 10.1007/s13132-014-0192-9.

Hayter, C. and Parker, M. (2019) 'Factors that influence the transition of university postdocs to non-academic scientific careers: an exploratory study,' *Research Policy*, 48(3), pp. 556–570. doi: 10.1016/j.respol.2018.09.009.

Krook, A. (no date) 'The emotional aftermath of leaving academia, part 1: old and new colleagues.' Available at: https://annekrook.com/?page_id=751 [Accessed 12 March 2024].

Lawson, C. and Lopes-Bento, C. (2024) 'Miss or match? The impact of PhD training on job market satisfaction,' *Research Policy*, 53(3), 104945. doi: 10.1016/j.respol.2023.104945.

Li, H. and Horta, H. (2024). 'Exploring the identity development of PhD graduates transitioning to non-researcher roles,' *Higher Education Quarterly*, 78, pp. 421–435. doi: 10.1111/hequ.12452.

Paolo, A.D. and Mañé, F. (2016) 'Misusing our talent? Overeducation, overskilling and skill underutilisation among Spanish PhD graduates,' *The Economic and Labour Relations Review*, 27(4), pp. 432–452. doi: 10.1177/1035304616657479.

Skakni, I., Inouye, K. and McAlpine, L. (2022) 'PhD holders entering non-academic workplaces: organisational culture shock,' *Studies in Higher Education*, 47(6), pp. 1271–1283. doi: 10.1080/03075079.2021.1876650.

Tupper, H. and Ellis, S. (2020) *The Squiggly Career*. London: Penguin.

A final word

As we acknowledged early in this book, pivoting your career beyond academia may mean navigating uncertainty, complex emotions, and re-examination of your identity and purpose. I hope this book has reassured you that you are not alone, and that your skills, experiences, and values are not only valid, but are also valuable and widely transferable beyond academia. After all, redefining your professional identity is not an erasure, it's an evolution: an opportunity to focus on the parts of yourself that you can take with you from academia and apply elsewhere, rather than dwelling on what you might be leaving behind.

I hope the evidence we've covered in literature review and case studies has reassured you that transitioning your career beyond academia isn't about having things 'all figured out.' Gone are the days of linear career ladders and 'jobs for life:' as we have seen, modern careers are built through experimentation, iteration, and adjustment. Instead of asking the seemingly impossible question 'What do I want to do with my life?' you're hopefully now able to break down your career transition into more manageable steps, focusing on what you want to keep and change through your next move. This is, in fact, an

DOI: 10.4324/9781003589785-9

example of exactly the kind of agility needed to build a sustainable, rewarding career in an unpredictable world.

We have also seen how your academic journey has equipped you with far more than specialist subject knowledge. You are a problem-solver, a communicator, a self-starter: qualities increasingly valued by employers in a fast-changing world of work. Yes, you may need to reframe these skills in ways that resonate with audiences beyond academia, but you are by no means starting completely from scratch.

Working through this book will also hopefully have equipped you with tools to avoid the kind of passive job hunting that leaves so many researchers frustrated, doubting their relevance beyond their academic niche. This book has been designed to empower you to start conversations: to gather insider knowledge, and to cultivate relationships that might lead to opportunities that never make it onto a job board. Such conversations can help you uncover options, clarify your goals, and build the kind of professional community that makes career change feel not only possible, but even exciting.

When the time comes to start your career change conversations, remember that when talking to potential employers in other sectors, you need to go beyond simply telling them what you've done in academia. That doesn't necessarily mean that what you've done isn't enough. It means being sure to clearly explain why what you've done matters to them, and how it shows that you can help them to achieve their goals. This requires learning to see your experience from the employer's point of view. What are their challenges and needs? How can you help with these? Adapting how you communicate your abilities and achievements is a skill in itself, which you can hone through practice, feedback, and support. And if you still encounter employers with outdated assumptions about academics, don't let their reactions define your worth: focus your energy on those who are positive about what you bring, and by whom you are likely to feel valued.

Overall, I'd encourage you to get comfortable with the idea that you're unlikely to solve your entire life with your first role beyond academia. Your next job isn't a destination, it's a step on a journey that will teach you more about yourself and your priorities. As we discussed in Chapter 7, the early stages of any transition can feel disorienting and overwhelming. You may even question whether you made the right choice. The key is to continue using the career management skills you've developed from this book to assess whether these feelings are genuine signals that your new conditions aren't right for you, or whether they are part of the process. Use tools like your keep/lose/add framework to regularly assess how your work aligns with your preferences and needs. Stay curious by exploring internal opportunities; look for ways to use the bits of yourself that you most want to, and to connect with like-minded peers. And most importantly, grant yourself time to grow into your new role(s) and environment. As difficult as this may be when transitioning from academia, avoid putting pressure on yourself to be an expert straight away. It's unlikely that employers or clients will expect this, and if they do, this may give you useful information as to whether they are in fact the people you want to be working with longer term.

Finally, remember that you are not doing this in isolation. Academia often encourages us to be solitary and self-critical, pitting us in competition with each other. When it comes to career change, however, connection, reflection, and mutual support are crucial. As we've seen throughout this book, job searches are influenced not solely by your capabilities, but by structural factors beyond your control including bias, unequal access to networks, and economic uncertainty. Support from trusted others can help you to avoid viewing rejection as a judgement on your self-worth. Whilst alumni careers support varies widely depending on where you are based, it is always worth investigating what support may be available through your current or previous institution. Also, as we saw in the 'useful resources' listed in Chapter 1, there is a growing global community of former academics who have forged fulfilling careers in range of different sectors. Seek them out, learn from them, and, as one last ask from me, consider sharing your journey if you feel comfortable doing so. Talk about the challenges as well as the achievements. By doing this, you're giving back to the community: showing others that change is possible, offering hope to those who are at the start of their transition, even if the path isn't always smooth.

When we exchange knowledge and stories in this way, we challenge the notion that success is purely an individual pursuit. Instead, we treat career transitions as a collective act of care and community. By working together, we can make journeys beyond academia clearer and kinder for those who come after us.

Because there is life – and meaningful work – beyond academia, and you are more than capable of finding it.

Index

Note: **Bold** page numbers refer to tables and page numbers followed by 'n' refer to notes.

abstract cognitive skills 63
academic-adjacent careers 72, 73
academic culture 3, 193–194
academic job markets 2–3
academic writing 162
AI 67, 71–72, 80, 164
Alice 200–202
Alice (PhD History) 144–145
alumni careers support 216
Amundsen, C. 40
Applicant Tracking Systems (ATS) 164

Bertrand, M. 122
Beyond The Thesis with Papa PhD (podcast): 105
Boyd, R. 188
breaking down skills **75–76**
Brendan's case study **79,** 82–83
Bryan, B. 194
Burnett, B. 92

Cadbury, Sir Dominic 38
career: change 43, 22, 158, 214; decisions 86–94; management skills 215; planning 37, 39, 58; theory 39; transition 7, 15, 185, 213; *see also individual entries*
Careers in Your Ears (podcast) 105
career options beyond academia: deciding on your options 23, 87–92; how to generate ideas 68; how to research options 7–8, 65–74; options linked to public engagement 50–51; options linked to research 48–50; options linked to teaching 47–48
career-related anxiety 16
career-related conversations 86–87, 214

Carlos 205–207
Carlos's story–focusing on research in industry 54
Cat 202–204
Caterine, Chris 158
Chaos Theory of Careers (CTC) 39
common questions about careers beyond academia 85–114; case study 87–92; job hunting timelines 97–107; making career decisions 86–94; making connections 94–97
communication: academic writing 162; open 211; skills 158, 161–162
community 31–32, 187
competition 2–3
contemporary career theories 58
coping with imposterism 193–195
cover letter 165–167, 177–179
cruel optimism 18
cultural differences (in networking) 131
culture shock 186
cumulative effect 154
CV 152, 161–162, 170–176

Dalgleish, Melissa 4
data analysis skills 69–70, 81
decoding job adverts 108–114
Designing Your Life (Burnett and Evans) 92

Ellis, S. 190
Elvidge, L. 97
Emma (PhD in Biochemical Engineering) 142
employers beyond academia 151–182; ;; goals or problems 156–157, 159–164; identifying 'friendly employers' 168–170; perceptions of PhDs and postdocs 143–144; perspectives 153–154; recalibrating your message for 158–159; recruitment methods used 6, 119, 121, 123, 136; showing your motivation to 165–168; speaking the employer's language 155–156; values and priorities 155, 157; value system 159
employer's expectations 98–99
equity issues 120, 133–134, 147
Evans, D. 92
existential crisis 17
exploring career options **11–12**, 65–74

filling vacancies 118–121, 148n1
full-time academic job 49

Global North 2–3, 118
Google Alert 128–129
graduate-level roles 108–111
graduate schemes 108–111
Guccione, K. 194

Hanan's case study **78,** 82
Hankel, Isaiah 152
Hayter, C. 186
hiring candidates 118; advertising vacancies online 121–122; informal 119, 121; internal hiring 118; online marketing methods 121; referrals 118; smoother transition 118; word-of-mouth hiring 119
hybrid (combining academic and other) careers 28

Ibarra, Herminia 22, 43
imposterism 193–195
internal hiring 118
internal opportunities 215
internship 129
interviews 156, 179–181

job: advertisements 122, 160, 170–171; crafting 190–192; decoding job adverts 108–114; level of 111–114; for life 213; major elements 111–112; mission 112; responsibilities of 160; role requirements 160; subject area 111; work activities 112
job hunting beyond academia 116, 147, 148n1, 214; activities 105, 136–139, **137–138**; as an international researcher 106–107; level of job to target 111–113; manage time pressures in 104–105; methods 134–136, **135,** 136, **137–138**; mixed-methods 124, 139, 147, 148; research process 124; timeline 97–107

keep/lose/add profile 44–51, **45,** 67, 93, 125–126, 196, **198–199,** 210, 211, 215; public engagement 50–51; research 48–50; teaching 46–48
knowledge: of academic attitudes 63; subject 62–64; subject-specialist 62; subject-specific 65–66; types of 64
Krook, Anne 187–188, 190

Leaving Academia (Caterine) 158
Letter or statement evolution 176–179
limiting beliefs 17, 60
LinkedIn 94–96, 117, 126, 127, 169; alumni 130, 163, 169–170; identify and follow/connect with people 130; people search 127

making the 'wrong choice' 93
McAlinden, S. 188
McAlpine, L. 40
mental and emotional barriers 5, 15–27
mixed-methods job hunt 139
Moses, Ashley 117, 132
motivation 165–167
moving on from academia 15–33
Mullainathan, S. 122

negative thoughts 22–23, **24–25**
Nelly 207–210
Nelly (PhD Modern Greek Studies) 145–147
networking/making professional connections 105, 117–118, 121, 136, 139, 140–141, 192
new start beyond academia 185–211; adapting to new ways of working 193; case study 197–209; exploring options from the inside 192; job crafting 190–192; physical and social conditions 195–196

online: communities 32, 34, 163; content 117; job adverts 121–122; marketing methods 121
opportunities 116–148; addressing limited networks and equity issues 133–134; case studies 139–147; costs 113; creating a role for yourself 131–133; filling vacancies 118–119; hiring candidates 118; internal hiring 118, 215; keeping/adding specific skills, knowledge, work activities 125–126; linked to specific sector/mission, finding roles 126–128; how researchers identify 116–117; specific location, finding roles in 130–131; specific organisation of interest, finding roles in 128–129; with stakeholders 125; through consulting 132
Organisation for Economic Co-operation and Development (OECD) 2, 13n1
overqualification 154, 165–168

Parker, M. 186
part-time work 129
Persson, Tina 152
physical and social conditions 195–196
planned happenstance 39, 40
policy-based roles 47
precarity 3
problem-solving skills 71
professional identity 17, 28, 73, 189, 191, 213
psychological and emotional barriers (to career change) 16–19, 21, 33
public engagement 50–51
pull factors 4

recruitment processes beyond academia 98–99, 100–103; 123, 147, 151; agencies 128; bias and discrimination 216; cover letters 165–167, 177–179; CVs 152, 161–162, 170–176; interviews 156, 179–181; methods 6, 136; perspective 113–114, 175–176; referrals 118;

risks involved 123, 134–136, 137–138; smoother transition 118
referrals 118
research-based jobs 48–50, 58
research skills 66–68, 81
resume 152
right decision 93
risks involved in recruitment processes 123, 134–136, 137–138

salary 107, 112–113, 168
search engine 37
searching job boards 57
sector-specific job boards and resources 128
self-advocacy 23, 195–196
self-narrative 22
Showforth (PhD and two postdocs in Microbiology) 143–144
Showforth's story–shifting academic skills into freelancing 55–56
skills 19, 60–83, 154, 155, 182; abstract cognitive 63; articulating your skills effectively to employers beyond academia 60–64; breaking down **75–76**; broader transferable 70–72, 81; career management 215; case study 77–80, **78–79**; communication 158; data analysis 69–70, 81; generating career ideas linked to your skills 74; and interests 77; knowledge of academic attitudes 63; navigating academic systems 81; non-technical roles 61–62; problem-solving 71; research skills and methods 66–68, 81; soft 176; subject knowledge and 64; subject-specific knowledge 65–66, 81; technical 64; transferable 61, 63; types of 64, 75, 81; understanding of how research and universities work 72–73; understanding your skills 18; using specialist equipment and technologies 68–69; valued beyond academia 64
small research grants (SRGs) 53
social identity theory 157
soft skills 176
Spotting career connections 77–79, **78–79**
squiggly career 40, 42
Squiggly Careers (Tupper and Ellis) 190
stereotypes 168–170, 182
student-facing work 48
subject knowledge 62–66, 81
support statement 22–23, 26–27

Tajfel, Henri 157
Tania's story–keeping up research 'on the side' 52–53
Tardelli, Matteo 152
teaching 46–48

technical ability 62, 63
technical skills 64
tenure track 3
terminology 9–10
transferable skills 61, 63, 186
transition beyond academia 37–58; case studies 51–57; evidence 38–41; 'keep/lose/add' profile 44–51, **45**; path 37, 40; plan 37; squiggly career 40, 42; staying in academia 58
Tupper, H. 190
Tyrrell, Naomi 1

uncover opportunities 128–129

value: position 17; system 159
volunteering 128

word-of-mouth hiring 117, 119, 147
working beyond academia: adapting to new working environments 189; culture shock 186; starting a new job 196